The Angel of Hadley

JAMES A. FREEMAN

The Angel of Hadley

A Thrilling Story of Rescue
in Colonial Massachusetts

WHITE RIVER PRESS
Amherst, Massachusetts

The Angel of Hadley

James A. Freeman

© 2009 James A. Freeman. All rights reserved.

A PUBLICATION OF HADLEY'S 350TH CELEBRATION

White River Press
P.O. Box 3561
Amherst, MA 01004

www.whiteriverpress.com

Printed in the United States of America

ISBN: 978-1-935052-25-8

Front cover: Detail from Frederick Chapman's 1850 painting, "The Angel of Hadley" or "The Perils of our Forefathers." Forbes Library, Northampton, MA.

Layout and cover design by Patricia Nobre

Library of Congress Cataloging-in-Publication Data

Freeman, James A., 1935-
 The angel of Hadley : a thrilling story of rescue in colonial Massachusetts, with sources, illustrations and bibliography / James A. Freeman.
   p. cm.
 Includes bibliographical references and index.
 ISBN 978-1-935052-25-8 (pbk. : alk. paper)
1. Hadley (Mass.)--History. 2. Hadley (Mass.)--Legends. 3. Massachusetts--History--Colonial period, ca. 1600-1775. 4. Goffe, William, 1605?-1679?--Legends. I. Title.
 F74.H1F743 2009
 974.4'23--dc22

To my real-life angels: Margaret, Eric, Maya, Nico and Kai

Figure 1: "General Goffe Repulsing the Indians at Hadley." Artist: Edward Henry Corbould (1815-1905); Engraver: James Stephenson (1808-86). William Henry Bartlett (1809-54), *The History of the United States of North America From the Discovery of the Western World to the Present Day* (New York: George Virtue, [?1860] 1.between pages 154-55).

Contents

Thank You

No historian works alone. Gathering so much data to explain the Angel of Hadley necessitated the help of many capable and amiable people. At first, the project seemed relatively simple: give a talk about the famous old man who supposedly rescued townspeople from an Indian attack in 1675. The occasion was a notable conference about "Hadley in the Seventeenth Century" at the Renaissance Center of the University of Massachusetts, Amherst, 3 May 2003, coordinated by the current and former Chairs of the Hadley Historical Commission, Marla Miller and my always supportive wife Margaret Freeman. My words elicited some surprisingly vigorous inquiries about the story's validity.

Thus the first thanks go to those attentive questioners as well as fellow residents of Hadley who later saw the video and contacted me. The more I researched, the more I realized the complexity of determining whether the tale had any basis in fact. Thus, I here thank the effort of so many others who helped gather the data you will soon encounter. Merely listing them cannot adequately compensate them for their generous support. Still, I hope they sense some measure of my gratitude. Gary Aho, Professor Emeritus, University of Massachusetts; Joseph Black, Professor, University of Massachusetts; Gerry Devine, former Chair, Hadley Select Board; James Kelly, Librarian, University of Massachusetts; Martha Noblick, Librarian, Historic Deerfield, Massachusetts; Elizabeth Pope, Librarian, American Antiquarian Society, Worcester; Mitzi Sawada, Professor Emerita, Hampshire College; Mary Thayer, Chair, Hadley 350th Committee; Ron Welburn, Professor, University of Massachusetts; the ever efficient Interlibrary Loan staff of the UMass library; the equally cooperative librarians in the Amherst College Archives, especially Marian Walker. Any errors probably sprang from me and will be gratefully corrected.

A Note to the Reader

Like you, I have been intrigued by the Angel of Hadley. Did the Puritan general William Goffe really save the frontier town from an attack by Native Americans near the end of the seventeenth century? We know that Goffe, born around 1610, was one of the 59 judges who signed the death warrant for the Stuart king Charles I in 1649. When Charles II, son of the executed king, returned to London during 1660 after exile in France, he proscribed Goffe and other regicides. His agents caught and killed several judges. Goffe prudently fled from England with two other supporters of Oliver Cromwell (1599-1658), his father-in-law, Lieutenant General Edward Whalley (c.1607-c.1675), and John Dixwell (1607-1689). First they found shelter in Boston, then New Haven and finally the West Street parsonage of Reverend John Russell (1625-1692), one of Hadley's first settlers. If relations with Indians had not deteriorated, the first two fugitives might have lived out their lives in merciful obscurity, protected by co-religionists. Historians agree about these facts.

However, long-standing tensions ignited in King Philip's War during the 1670s and Anglo settlers suffered assaults by Natives. The original inhabitants often rightly resented the newcomers' violence, greed and intolerance. Hadley's neighbors like Hatfield, Northampton and Deerfield lived in fear. The colonizers nervously recorded each attack and longed for a leader to rescue them. Again, historians can verify these raids throughout the region.

You probably already know the outlines of the incident that earned Goffe his title of Angel. As the story goes, in our small frontier town during early September 1675, the congregation had gathered in the meeting house to pray for protection from Indians. Suddenly, an old man with a long white beard and outmoded clothing burst into the service. He warned the Hadley folk that skirmishers were about to attack, organized a successful defense and promptly vanished, never again to be seen. During an era that believed supernatural beings, good and evil, interacted with human beings – the town would soon persecute Molly Webster as a witch – the appearance of this champion elated them. He resembled Old Testament heroes, Moses, say, and Joshua and Gideon and Samson. Those worthies had delivered another chosen people in the past; so too this elderly commander reassured the current faith community during its darkest hour that Deity had not abandoned them.

Now for the mystery. Such a miracle would have exhilarated all New England settlers. Yet no contemporary mentioned it. None of the dutifully literate Puritans recorded the dramatic rescue in any book, diary, letter or official report. Not until nearly a century later did anyone describe the deed. A tentative footnote in former governor Thomas Hutchinson's 1765 history book first declared that this savior was Major General William Goffe. Later authors like Sir Walter Scott, James Fenimore Cooper, Nathaniel Hawthorne and Robert Southey quickly elaborated the incident. They transformed the flesh-and-blood man into a symbol who could supply the new nation with some proud memories.

Twenty-first century audiences must admit they have two different kinds of reality to process. They can contemplate the bravery and pathos of the historical Goffe. He helped depose Charles I but later fell from his position in Cromwell's administration to the role of escapee and near captive in the Russells' secret room. Like a character in a tragedy, he spent his remaining years cut off from autonomy, light and society, writing coded letters to his wife in

England, whom he never again saw. At the same time, readers must wonder whether the glorious rout of enemies attributed to Goffe-the-Angel ever happened. Is the second Goffe a mythical being? The stirring reversal of Hadley's fortune he effected on that amazing fall day, so compelling to the nineteenth century, obviously sounds to twenty-first century readers like a convenient foundation legend, perhaps racist, obviously comforting to its many believers.

The following pages provide you with much material to understand who the verifiable Goffe was, why he came to New England, how his peers viewed the world and, most important, how later generations insisted that same figure had saved Hadley. Each section is nearly self-contained so you may go to those topics that interest you.

Admittedly, so many facts presented in such a short form may overwhelm you. I deliver them with the benign intention of supplying all the background that a student of the Angel will need to decide about his authenticity. For ease of comprehension, I urge you to divide the words and pictures into two related categories. One, what kind of imaginative world did people living before us inhabit? Their hopes and prejudices, so often and so vigorously repeated, show how persistent are questions we still face. These issues concern obedience to authority, pride in our own heritage, deprecation of others' values, need to bend facts so our side triumphs and wisdom of colonizing someone else's land. A related category concerns the ways that artists have adapted the rescue story to so many uses. We might compare these partial views to the famous image of blind people describing an elephant: to one, its tail means an elephant resembles a rope, to another, its side communicates a wall, to a third, its leg announces a column, still another believes the ear resembles a sail. The imaginative reincarnations of the historical Goffe testify to the story's perennial appeal and should excuse their deviations from any possible reality.

One word of caution: regretfully, almost all written records from Goffe's time attacked anyone who differed from the writers' political, social and religious views. Their vocabulary was usually binary and non-negotiable: us versus them. The Puritans felt no restraint when they insulted monarchists, Native Americans, Catholics and other Protestant sects. To be fair, we should note that their foes used the same inflammatory idiom against them. Such mutual antagonism reminds us that in Goffe's era tolerance for diversity was not an ideal. Our Puritan ancestors, so valiant in their struggle to survive, continually felt under siege. Therefore, they responded with aggressive words and occasional acts of genocide against Indians. They felt they were obeying the biblical encouragement for holy war, for either conversion or destruction of those who did not resemble them.

During King Philip's War, they honed bitter clichés that persisted long after actual threats had lessened. Goffe would have understood that the Natives were commonly accused of having a "Quarrelsom disposition and Perfidious Carriage"; continuing on, they were "Barbarous, Savage and Heathenish Natives," malevolent and dangerous. (Brief and True Narration 1675, title page) Even nine decades after the conflict, a fair-minded academic who tried to balance the moral deficiencies of both English and Indian fighters had to list the usual slurs employed by newcomers: "Dogs, caitiffs, miscreants and hell-hounds." (Belknap 1784)

Certainly, they were not monsters (as some Victorian writers claimed). Their fear may explain why no one reported Hadley's rescue for a hundred years. Britain ruled the colonists throughout the eighteenth century. Even years after the regicide, townspeople might have kept silent because they worried about punishment from London. The law had a long memory.

Independent citizens of the post-1776 nation, though, wanted to advertise and praise their own past. Subscribing to the theory that great individuals created our country, they selected agreeable incidents from a leader's life (Columbus' perseverance) and neglected unflattering traits (his religious zealotry, avarice and slaughter of natives). Many times, nineteenth-century American authors reinvented their Puritan ancestors by dramatizing their epic struggle against the pitiless "red" foes. We must expect bigoted remarks as a persistent part of the heroic Angel tale.

The Legend of the
Angel of Hadley

Three celebrities from Hadley illustrate the ways that historical truth and social need may create a memorable legend. At one end of a credibility spectrum, we have verifiable information about Joseph B. Hooker (1814-1879). Born on West Street at the site now marked by a commemorative boulder, he graduated from Hopkins Academy and West Point, then became a famous general in the Civil War, one whose reputation has varied over the years. On the far end of possibility, John Dunbar (1841-1914) also lived on West Street before the Civil War with his relatives, the Smiths. Having graduated from Hopkins Academy, Dunbar attended Amherst College, served in the Union army and, after the conflict, became an advocate for the Pawnees. Perhaps he inspired Michael Blake's fictional John Dunbar, the hero of *Dances With Wolves*. (Freeman 2009) Positioned between facts and speculations, we have William Goffe, the Angel of Hadley.

Once the United States broke free from England, it needed home-grown heroes. It first adopted George Washington as its icon, endlessly picturing him on canvas, dinner plates and wallpaper. The War of 1812, the Creek War and the depredations of Barbary pirates encouraged a siege mentality that eagerly idolized successful commanders like Andrew Jackson and Stephen Decatur. Yet even those worthies could not satisfy the hunger for a savior who would reassure beleaguered former colonists that history had in the past and would in the future protect them from enemies. England had King Arthur, waiting in Avalon until his country required him; France had Charlemagne; Germany, Frederick Barbarossa; Denmark, Holger. North Americans had to discover ancestors who could rise to the awesome level of myth.

Ironically, an opponent of our Revolution, Hutchinson, the former Tory Governor of Massachusetts, introduced the story of the magical rescuer of Hadley. For him, Goffe the regicide warned that rebels would be punished. Soon novelists, historians and poets retold the stirring tale. Nationalist writers contradicted Hutchinson because Goffe opposed Charles' tyranny and Indian barbarism just as they had recently combated George III and other foes. The Angel provided that model of bravery, skill and self-denial essential for citizens in a fresh but hostile world. Still other writers offered Goffe as a bit of picturesque local color.

The next pages urge you to ponder both the historical Goffe and the (perhaps) legendary Angel. You may conclude that the two were really one person. Probably, though, the rescuer will always be a Rorschach figure that anyone can characterize because he never existed. We can agree that Americans from the late 1700s onward needed a hero like the Angel.

Figure 2: "William Goffe." Fiske 1890, page 220. Similar picture in Bolton 1919, page 395.

Hadley in the
Seventeenth Century

Before we see how subsequent tellers changed Hutchinson's original Hadley anecdote to suit different purposes, let us recall the imaginative world of seventeenth-century colonists. Their minds seethed with hopes, fears and suspicions. Protestants mistrusted Catholics, and vice versa; Puritan sects quarreled with one another; Commonwealth "Roundheads," supporters of Oliver Cromwell and his Puritan regime, disliked Royalist "Cavaliers"; and white settlers battled Native Americans, whom they sneeringly called "Indians," "savages" (dwellers in the *silva*, or woods), "barbarians" (people who spoke no real language), "pagans" (inhabitants of a *pagus*, or outlying district), "villains" (those who live near a *villa*, or country house) and "heathen" (wanderers on the empty heath). Not every newcomer shared these pugnacious beliefs, but we must sadly say they were the mainstream credos. Like beleaguered gladiators in the hostile arena of this world, Goffe's generation had to be uncompromising.

To give ourselves a context for the Angel story and to understand the reasons it became one of our nation's best-known incidents, let us ask a series of questions: Why did Puritans leave England? Why were they in New England? What did they think of personal sin? What did they think of other religions? What did they think of monarchy? What did they think of Indians? Once we have heard their opinions, we can begin to speculate why, if Goffe actually saved Hadley, townspeople would cover up the extraordinary deed. If he did not rescue the settlers, why did the legend spread so widely after our separation from Britain? Finally, is it possible to decide between what really happened and what we wish happened?

Why did the Puritans
Leave England?

Hadley became a town in 1659. However, events following Henry VIII's break with the Roman Catholic Church in the 1530s shaped its inhabitants' world view. The Tudor king's declaration of independence from the Vatican meant that English could seek personal connection to God by appointing their own clergy, reading the Bible in their own language and simplifying liturgy. Britain soon became home to dozens of sects, each claiming direct inspiration from the Deity and endangering political stability. Mary (1516-1558), a devout Catholic, savagely repressed the Protestants and set the stage for civil insurrection. Elizabeth I (1533-1603) established the Anglican Church as an institution that moderate citizens could support. She saw it as an instrument to end internal bickering and defend against foreign enemies. Still, many sincere worshippers dissented from High Church practices. Some unobtrusively remained Catholic; others wanted to purify the new church from reminders of the old faith (the Puritans); yet others chose to leave the new church entirely (the Separatists, or Pilgrims). Members of both these latter groups felt that the newly established national church in England was still too "papistical" and wanted freedom to recreate the community of the first disciples as described in the book of Acts. Consequently, many fled across the Atlantic to North America.

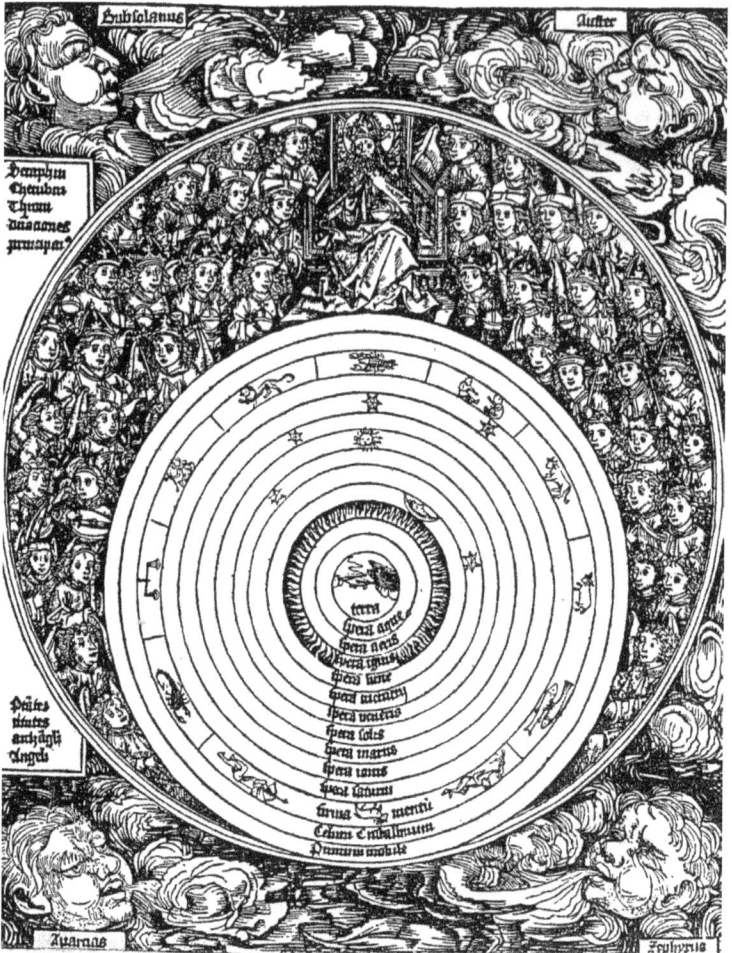

Figure 3: "The Universe Governed by God." Nuremberg 1493.

During the thousand years when one church ruled Europe, doctrines and practices changed, but people could look to it for stability. This typical late medieval view summarized the reassuringly tidy assumption. The four winds at the corners blow on (literally, "inspire") the universe while God, his heavenly court and nine orders of angels (their names on left: "seraphs, cherubs, thrones") enclose the planets, firmament, fixed stars and "first mover" (*primum mobile*). The earth (*terra*) nestles in the center of an ordered cosmos. All components have a specific place and work together to honor God.

Figure 4: "Elizabeth I as Part of the Natural Order of the Universe." Case 1588, frontpiece.

The Protestant Reformation challenged the earlier ideal of one privileged church. Catholics and disciples of Martin Luther fought one another with both words and weapons, hoping to reassert control. Their differences prompted eloquent reasoning and scurrilous vituperation.

Issued by an articulate reformer, this learned book of political theory offered a new model of the cosmos. It supported Aristotle's claim that only just states flourish, a seemingly defensible premise. However, the illustration must have upset Romans and

Puritans alike. Elizabeth, an earthly monarch, has supplanted God as pictured in the previous engraving. The microcosm of the English monarchy now coincided with the macrocosm of a Ptolemaic universe. Attached to individual transparent spheres, planets revolved about unmoving *Justitia*. Identified by their astrological signs, the moon, Mercury, Venus, Earth, the sun, Mars, Jupiter and Saturn fan out to the realm of the fixed stars. Each heavenly body connects to a virtue ("Fertility, Skill, Mercy, Religion, Strength, Prudence and Majesty"). Both image and text imply that Elizabeth I controls nature, morals and, by extension, a state church. However symmetrical this plan of the universe may be, the fiercely individualistic non-Anglicans felt left out of such a grand alliance between astronomy, ethics and monarchy.

No matter what non-conformists felt about the revised world plan, they had to admit there were signs of its truth. In 1588, a mighty squall, which they felt God commanded, scattered the enormous Spanish armada that had sailed from Catholic Spain to invade the island. This rescue relieved Britons and emphasized the pattern in history that Goffe's age inherited: outsiders will menace a just people, but Deity may save his chosen ones by means of an inspired leader.

What did the Puritans in
New England Believe?

The New World seemed to be an ideal location for non-Anglicans because of three reasons. They could build their own spiritual city on a hill, free from "popish" pressures of the state church, and labor with like-minded believers to save their souls. Also, they could help the natives who, according to the belief of the day, worshipped false gods and were ripe for conversion. Plus, Indians had goods to trade and territory to sell. Worship, conversion and exploitation lured dissenters here. They felt they could accomplish these worthy goals because they had a special relation with God. They continually lived in two eras, their own and that of their spiritual ancestors, the ancient Hebrews. As one minister explained in 1663, "[T]he cause of his people Israel was right from God, to keep gods Commandments in matters of Religion. This was the cause of God and Israel then, and I hope it will appear anon, that the very same is the cause of God and his people now." (Cause of God 1663, page 10)

In general, we can say that these mission-oriented emigrants shared four basic ideas about sin, other religions, monarchy and Indians.

1. Puritans were Deeply Concerned with Personal Sin

The hopeful immigrants may have changed their location, expecting to cultivate the new land and its inhabitants. Unfortunately, they carried with them old world hostilities that encouraged personal and external conflicts. Perhaps self-loathing best characterizes the dissenters' psychological temperament. They disliked their own innate sinfulness, fearing that it would damn them to eternal perdition. Unlike Catholics, who accepted various sacraments to purge sin, Puritans felt that most human actions estranged them from a just God. His mercy alone, not their deeds, would preserve a few individuals from hellfire. Many of them examined themselves and current events for any sign that they might be among the elect.

THE BIBLE
AND
HOLY SCRIPTVRES
CONTEYNED IN
THE OLDE AND NEWE
Teftament.

TRANSLATED ACCOR-
ding to the Ebrue and Greke, and conferred With
the beft tranflations in diuers langages.

WITH MOSTE PROFITABLE ANNOTA-
tions vpon all the hard places, and other things of great
importance as may appeare in the Epiftle to the Reader.

FEARE YE NOT.STAND STIL, AND BEHOLDE
the faluacion of the Lord, which he wil fhewe to you this day. Exod.14,13.

THE LORD SHAL FIGHT FOR YOU: THEREFORE
holde you your peace, Exod. 14, vers.14.

AT GENEVA.
PRINTED BY ROVLAND HALL
M. D. L X.

Figure 5: Geneva Bible 1560, title page.

The major mechanism for communication between God and solitary, needy humans took place via the Bible. It furnished Puritans with an invaluable ladder upward toward heaven and away from the dangerous earth. This vernacular translation had to be made abroad. When Mary ascended the English throne in 1553 with her plans to exterminate non-Catholics, many of the endangered dissenters fled to the continent, mainly to Holland, Germany and Switzerland. John Foxe wrote his *Book of Martyrs* (1563) at Basel to commemorate those Protestants whom Mary executed. Other learned nonconformists took advantage of the relatively open presses in Frankfurt and Strasbourg to criticize Catholicism. Typically, the non-Anglican sects began to disagree among themselves, a habit they would carry across the Atlantic. Led by John Knox, a sizable group relocated to Geneva, still under the influence of Jean Calvin. The Swiss city attracted scholars who translated directly from the Bible's original Hebrew and Greek, not, as Catholics were required to do, from Jerome's late fourth-century Latin. After two years, the gifted linguists produced this version in 1560. It quickly became the most popular one in Britain. Because Protestants wanted to decode the Bible directly, the editors supplied elaborate notes and illustrations.

This title page emphasized the close connection that Protestants felt with Old Testament Hebrews. In the foreground, pursuing Egyptians close in on fleeing and unarmed former slaves as they follow Moses to a promised land. In front of them, the Red Sea seems to be impassable, but a distant pillar of fiery smoke (symbol of Yahweh) reminds the faithful that God will transport them away from misbelievers over mighty waters to Israel. The marian persecutions paralleled Pharaoh's, driving believers across the English Channel and the Atlantic.

Hadley today is lucky to possess a 1599 edition of the Geneva Bible. It belonged to Dorothy Russell, wife of Pastor John Russell. (Freeman 2003) Perhaps it solaced Goffe during his years of hiding in their parsonage. If Goffe used it, one feature suggests a sad emotional possibility. He never again saw his wife, Whalley's daughter, and had to communicate with her back in England by smuggled letters. The most worn pages in the Hadley Bible are those of the Old Testament Song of Songs. That book celebrates physical love, the pain of separation and a final joyous marriage, all topics painfully close to the lonely man hiding in Reverend Russell's secret room. We can hope that the Song helped Goffe deal with his cruel isolation.

2. Puritans Mistrusted Other Religions

In addition to lamenting about their own toxic sins, Puritans abhorred other religions. Modern goals like moderation, inclusivity, diversity, acceptance and tolerance to them connoted surrender to false values of this world, the flesh and the Devil. In Europe, they rejected the broad minded Dutch, who offered asylum, because the Netherlands had to balance kindness toward refugees against prudent relations with James I. Occasionally, Holland complied with requests from London to extradite English dissidents.

Scripture, Puritans felt, not secular compromises, offered all things needful to the earnest seeker for direct relation with the Deity. Ideally, it would provide a beacon to light the same path for every reader. But all humans were fallen heirs to the prattling mob at Babel and thus had lost the right reason required for uniform comprehension. Quickly there arose as many interpretations as there were readers. Even in the early years of the Reformation, Jean Calvin predicted idiosyncratic readings: "[T]here will be a pliant, and as it were, many-coloured Gospel, for we see how everyone flatters himself and is disposed to follow his own appetites." (Calvin 1564)

The Anabaptist   *The Brownist*

The Familist   *The Papist*

Figure 6: "A Whip for the Back of a Backsliding Brownist." Crouch 1640. Four groups that Puritans considered mistaken readers of the Bible rowdily toss it in a blanket. Anabaptists rejected infant baptism; Robert "Troublechurch" Browne (c. 1550-1633) led an idiosyncratic sect; Familists claimed salvation came from faith alone; Papists (Roman Catholics) had a long tradition of exegesis that, like dogma of other groups, justified their own practices.

Figure 7: Illustration from *The Lamentations of Germany.* Vincent 1638, page 9.

Many inflammatory sectarian propaganda tracts flooded from presses during the Thirty Years War (1618-1648). Here, the victims are Protestants, but both sides committed unspeakable atrocities. One 23-year old Protestant crusader, Duke Christian of Brunswick, bragged that he had devastated nearly fifty Catholic towns and castles in Westphalia and Hesse. The extraordinary fury of these religious wars on the Continent emphasized the uneasy conviction that an annoyed God was using people of alien faiths to punish sinners. Goffe's contemporaries sometimes tried to make sense of their woes by assuming they deserved divine reprimand. Still, they wanted a leader who could repel enemies.

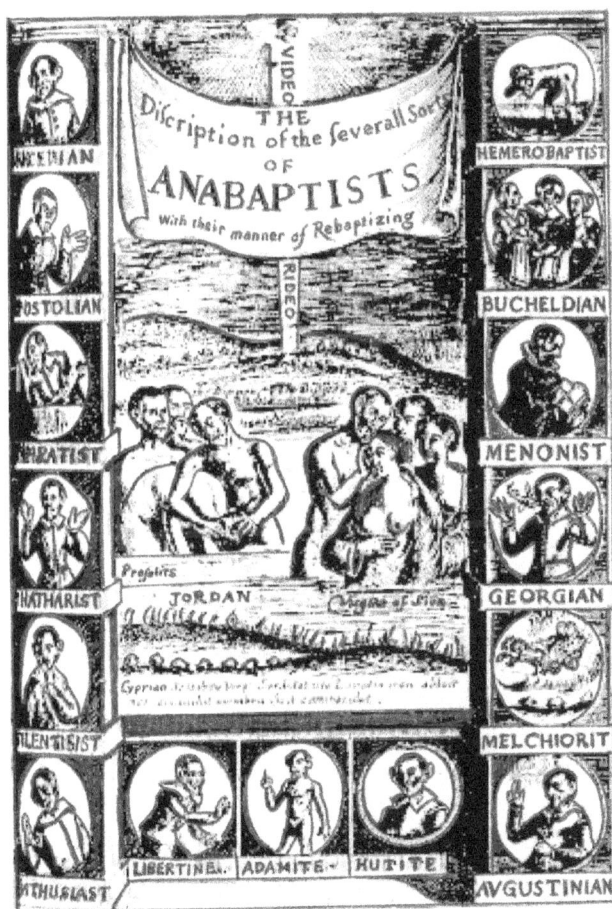

Figure 8: Illustration for The Dippers Dipt. Featley 1647, page 25.

The picture spotlights some of the many cults that sprang up outside the more traditional denominations such as Lutheran, Anglican and Presbyterian. Baptism divided believers. They wrangled over questions of immersion or sprinkling and infant or adult baptism. The central panel shows mature "Prosolits" and "Virgins of Sion" being submerged in the Jordan. The fifteen thumbnails name fringe sects ("Bucheldian, Melchorit, Apostolian"). Their doctrinal squabbles hindered the ideal of Christian and English unity, perhaps making them vulnerable to the highly organized Catholics. They prompt a banner from heaven that comments, *Video Rideo*, "I see and I laugh."

Even after Goffe's Parliamentarians won the Civil War (1642-1651), Puritans understood how many alternate beliefs still opposed them. The Old Testament ideal of biological family (*mishpacha*) and the New Testament goal of spiritual community (*koinonía*) eluded Protestants. Congregations continually quarreled among themselves. Driven by concern for their souls

Figure 9: Illustration for "A Catalogue of the Several Sects and Opinions in England." Catalogue 1647.

Perhaps Presbyterian ridicule, expressed in sarcastic rhymes on a broadside. By Goffe's day, defining correct belief had long been a major topic of commentators. Here the various groups range from Jesuits to Adamites, people who copied unfallen Adam by not wearing clothes, and Thraskites, who observed the Jewish Sabbath. Cromwell might have been sympathetic to the Seekers, but did not make any preference public.

after death, sincere people listened to their consciences and evolved different principles by which to sanctify their earthly existence.

When confronted with diverse opinions, antagonists often moved away from each other geographically. This habit of seeking a place where only compatible people would assemble puts in perspective the splits in congregations during the mid-1600s that led dissidents up the Connecticut Valley to establish Hadley and, even in that remote place, move a meeting house from its first site.

3. Puritans Disliked Monarchy

A third background point about Goffe and his Puritan cohorts explains why Hadley sheltered him illegally. Alongside personal sin and other creeds, they disliked monarchy. Ever since Henry VIII broke from the Roman Catholic Church in the early sixteenth century, those who remained loyal to the old belief alternated on the British throne with those who embraced Protestantism in some of its many forms. The Catholic "Bloody" Mary Tudor burned to death some 300 Protestants and many Puritans fled the land; Elizabeth I imposed her Anglican compromise, but it still did not satisfy everyone; James I (1566-1625) and Charles I (1600-1649) drew ever nearer to Rome. Charles even courted a Catholic wife on the Continent. These traditional kings alarmed reformers, who gagged at any whiff of hierarchy. Words like priest and bishop, elaborate ceremonies, decorated churches and showy vestments connoted Babylonian perversion of the Gospel and lawless repression of conscientious dissenters. The Civil War further encouraged partisans of the Stuarts and of Oliver Cromwell to equate government with religion. Generally, the crown depended on landed Anglo-Catholic country squires, while the Parliamentarians attracted city people, merchants and scholars. Each side demonized the other, a habit of mind that Goffe brought to America.

Figure 10: Englands Wolfe 1647.

The text accompanying this illustration for a Puritan broadside accused Prince Rupert's monarchist troops of looting. No one can prove whether crimes occurred or, if they did, whether Rupert had much to do with them. However, accuracy was never the goal of political attacks.

The Civil War ended when skilled generals like Goffe and Whalley outsoldiered the Cavaliers. The new Puritan administration insisted that Charles had not been a legitimate king but rather a tyrant and thus had no divine right to live. On 29 January 1648/9, 59 judges, including Cromwell, Goffe, Dixwell and Whalley (whose names are highlighted in the following chart), signed his death warrant.

Figure 11: The Death Warrant for Charles I .

A modern transcription of the Death Warrant for Charles I.

At the high Co[ur]t of Justice for the tryinge and judginge of Charles Steuart Kinge of England January xxixth Anno D[omi]ni 1648.

Whereas Charles Steuart Kinge of England is and standeth convicted attaynted and condemned of High Treason and other high Crymes, And sentence uppon Saturday last was pronounced against him by this Co[ur]t to be putt to death by the severinge of his head from his body Of w[hi]ch sentence execuc[i]on yet remayneth to be done, These are therefore to will and require you to see the said sentence executed In the open Streete before Whitehall uppon the morrowe being the Thirtieth day of this instante moneth of January between the houres of Tenn in the morninge and Five in the afternoone of the same day w[i]th full effect And for soe doing this shall be yo[u]r sufficient warrant And these are to require All Officers and Souldiers and other the good people of this Nation of England to be assistinge unto you in this service Given under o[ur] hands and Seales.

To Colonell Francis Hacker, Colonell Huncks and Lieutenant Colonell Phayre and to every of them.	Har. Waller	Hen. Smyth	A. Garland	Symon Mayne	Tho. Wogan
	John Blakiston	Per. Pelham	Edm. Ludlowe	Tho. Horton	John Venn
	M. Livesey	J. Hutchinson	Ri. Deane	Henry Marten	J. Jones	*Gregory Clement*
Jo. Bradshawe	John Okey	**Willi. Goffe**	Robert Tichborne	Vinct. Potter	John Moore	Jo. Downes
Tho. Grey	J. Da[n]vers	Tho. Pride	H. Edwardes	Wm. Constable	Gilbt. Millington	Tho. Wayte
O. Cromwell	Jo. Bourchier	Pe. Temple	Daniel Blagrave	Rich. Ingoldesby	G. Fleetwood	Tho. Scot
Edw. Whalley	H. Ireton	T. Harrison	Owen Rowe	Willi. Cawley	J. Alured	Jo. Carew
	Tho. Mauleverer	J. Hewson	Willm. Purefoy	Jo. Barkstead	Robt. Lilburne	Miles Corbet
			Ad. Scrope	Isaa. Ewer	Will. Say	
			James Temple	**John Dixwell**	Anth. Stapley	
				Valentine Wauton	Greg. Norton	
					Tho. Challoner	

Figure 12: Anonymous German artist, "The public Execution of Charles I in front of Whitehall."

The next day, in front of a large crowd, the executioner beheaded Charles. The medallions in the upper register portray from left to right: General Thomas Fairfax (1612-1671), Charles and Cromwell. Killing a monarch galvanized both factions for decades and illustrated the savage penalty of being in the wrong camp. Hostilities did not end on this day, as Goffe discovered.

Men of his era replicated the same pattern after combat on both continents: they killed as many of their foe as possible, vainly hoping execution would prevent future conflict. As soon as fighting in Massachusetts stopped, Richard Hutchinson announced, "The Warr in New-England visibly Ended. King Philip that Barbarous Indian now Beheaded." (Hutchinson 1677, title page)

Figure 13: "The Emblem of Englands Distractions." Fairthorne 1658.

Each side employed highly evocative symbolism to justify its position and excuse death sentences. This Puritan engraving promoted Oliver Cromwell as their ideal of a divinely chosen champion who had defeated secular and spiritual evil. Under the hovering dove of Peace, he tramples Error, who has lost her crown and rosary, and serpent-like Faction. Above them, Fame trumpets the victory. The right pillar, topped by Parliament, shows England, Scotland and Ireland presenting him the winner's tiara. The left pillar, erected on Mount Zion, honors "Constancy and Strength, the People's Salvation as the Supreme Law, Magna Charta." Two top vignettes recall God saving Noah and Isaac; lower vignettes demonstrate the benefits of peace when men turn spears into pruning hooks and swords into plows. Such a model government required a warfaring Christian like Cromwell. With scepter-like sword in one hand (impaling the crowns of the three kingdoms) and Bible in the other, he professes, MONO TO ΘEO ΔΟΞΑ, "Only God."

To combat Puritan propaganda, Royalists waged a pamphlet war against the Parliamentarians. The skill and virulence of these attacks showed how potent were the forces arrayed against men like Goffe when they were out of power. Resentment of past injuries seemed to grow over time. A motto Charles II added to the Scottish emblem warned, "No one hurts me with impunity."

Figure 14: ἘΙΚΩΝ ΒΑΣΙΛΙΚΗ [Eikon Basilike]. The True Pourtracture of His Sacred Majestie. MARSHALL 1649, frontpiece.

Although Charles was buried on 8 February, his memory as a martyr slaughtered by Puritan zealots remained alive in royalists' minds. This curious book appeared about the same day as his interrment. Supposedly written by Charles, the actual author was his chaplain John Gauden (1605-1662). Picturing the slain king as a pious and benevolent, although misunderstood, benefactor, the symbols parallel him with Christ alone in the garden. On the left, the palm tree that grows best when weighted down was allegorical shorthand to communicate virtue under adversity. Above the tree, the rock triumphs against the raging sea, fit emblem for a just ruler who cannot be swayed by the mob. From the clouded sky above tree and rock, a beam of light promises future clarity. Charles ponders a book that gives him hope by refuting the Puritans' claim that they alone properly interpret the Bible. Inspired, he looks upward and has a vision of blessedness and glory in heaven. *Gratia*, "divine grace," fills the crown of thorns he holds in his right hand, which replaces the cast-off earthly crown. Although clearly partisan fiction, *Eikon* so united opponents against the Commonwealth that John Milton felt compelled to answer it in November 1649 with a corrective monograph called *Eikonoklastes* ("The Image Breaker").

Figure 15: Woodcut of Harrison's Execution, 13 October 1660, near Charing Cross. Rebels No Saints 1661. Reproduced in Warren, 1873, page 145.

Words certainly had power, but after the Restoration of Charles II, the court sought physical vengeance, legal or not, against judges like Goffe. The barbaric execution of his fellow Puritan Thomas Harrison (1606-13 October 1660) emphasized the danger of any anti-Royalist expression, past or present. Harrison was not an obsessive adherent of Cromwell, but he and nine other judges suffered the horror of being drawn through the streets in a sledge, hanged until nearly dead, then cut down while still alive so the executioner could disembowel and decapitate them and then cut their bodies into four quarters. The diarist Samuel Pepys observed the butchery and commented that Harrison was "looking as cheerful as any man could do in that condition." (Pepys Pre-1669, page 55)

The Civil War continued. The anti-monarchists knew that they risked their lives whether they stayed in England or fled to America. A 1678 arrest warrant in America for Goffe still sounds ominous. (Plan 1678) Colonists' fear of reprisal supports the theory that Hadley remained silent about the presence of Goffe and Whalley for pious and practical reasons.

4. Puritans Distrusted Native Americans

A fourth locus of Puritan anxiety, in addition to sin, heterodoxy and kings: Indians. Once escaped from England to Massachusetts, most of the exiles mistrusted indigenous people as unpredictable creatures, not quite human, closer genetically to wild beasts than Europeans. Initially, the newcomers believed that these "primitive" peoples would become docile servants to a Christian god, to the whites and to a business economy. Soon both groups looked on the other as predators.

Charles I, desperate for revenue, chartered the Company in 1629 to produce income. Owners had to encourage investors by overcoming suspicion of the new-found territory's occupants. A decade before the Massachusetts Bay Company began, William Bradford recorded the misgivings his Separatist flock brought with them from Europe on the Mayflower. Personally, he was not particularly prejudiced and engineered good relations with tribes. Even before the Pilgrims landed at Cape Cod in November 1620, however, he wrote:

> It is recorded in scripture as a mercie to the apostle [Paul in Acts 28] and his shipwraked company, that the barbarians shewed them no smale kindness in refreshing them, but these savage barbarians [in America], when they mette with them (as after will appear) were readier to fill their sides full of arrows than otherwise. And for the season it was winter, and they know that the winters of that cuntrie know them to be sharp and violent, and subjecte to cruel and fierce stormes, deangerous to travill to known places, much more to serch an unknown coast. Besides, what could they see but a hideous and desolate wilderness, full of wild beasts and willd men. (Bradford Pre-1646, page 96)

This dark vision lightened when other reports appeared. Glowing descriptions touted America's free riches. William Morrell, an Anglican divine who spent two years in Plymouth during the early 1620s, listed the untapped natural resources: "the Bee ... berries ... The Filbert, Cherry, and the fruitful vine ... Cedar, Cypres, Spruce, and Beech ...Deare ... Museats [muskrats], Lynces, Otter, Bever ..Swans and Geese, Herne, Phesents, Duck & Crane." Morrell's talk of Fish and fertile fields and handsome Indian "women, which for th'most part are / Of comely forms," implied that one could again possess Paradise. (Morrell 1625, *passim*)

The Bay Company took advantage of ancient reveries that described Cocaigne or El Dorado. Its persuasive advertisement pictured an amiable "savage" who asked (in the words of Acts 16:9), "Come Over and Help Us." Promoting dreams of missionary and mercantile profit, the image invited investors to imagine a pacific inhabitant whose soul needed instruction and whose soil, easily surrendered, would yield abundant crops. Seen with the symbolic vision of the seventeenth century, the floral wreath can resemble a parade of bees, emblems of a purposeful, benign monarchy. By Goffe's day, just when King Philip massed his Indians, the Massachusetts Bay Council substituted a bare-breasted female, unrealistically implying that natives had become even more compliant. (At a Council Held at Boston 1678)

Figure 16: The Seal of the Massachusetts Bay Company.

A modern historian explained, "[T]he Massachusetts Bay Colony is to be a charitable project …: the native people will be 'helped.' From the 'darkness of heathenism' they will be drawn to the bright light of Protestant Christianity. From their lowly state of 'savagery' they will be raised to the heights of English 'civility.' … English settlers [will be] 'taming the wilderness' and remaking America in the image of their motherland." (Demos 1995, page 3)

How the Indians
Resisted the Anglos

Despite the land's fertility, the inhabitants proved to be neither passive nor naive. They often frustrated both missionary and mercantile goals. By the late seventeenth century, the mental resistance of Britons to the first inhabitants was as sturdy as the wooden palisades protecting many frontier towns. In the newcomers' religious sensibility, Indians resembled two loathed opponents. Like Old Testament Canaanites, they were inconvenient dwellers in territory they felt their Christian god had encouraged them to invade. It was a sanctuary for his elected people. A Victorian chronicled the emergence of Goffe from his hiding place with typical Puritan language: the old man "sallied forth to win yet one more victory over the hosts of Midian ere death should come to claim him in his woodland retreat." (Fisk 1880, reprint of 1898, page 245)

New England's indigenous people also replaced contemporary papists in the collective Anglo mind. Both dabbled in non-Christian superstition. The heathen who impeded the march of civilization made immigrants uneasy because when they paid attention to Christianity, they often listened to French Catholics. Even supposed converts to Protestantism, the Praying Indians, occasionally turned against their English mentors.

On a secular level, natives sometimes taught them to farm or sold them property. Despite the mission to improve the morals of others, few Englishmen objected to stealing Indian land or breaking treaties. When Roger Williams preached that only the natives, not the king of England, could grant land, the colony expelled him. Later historians admitted that conflict arose because white settlers commandeered territory. An often-reprinted school catechism reviewed the facts:

[Q]. What were the causes of the wars with the Indians?

[A]. They had sold their land to the white people, who had cleared it up and destroyed their game. (Tuttle 1864, page 5)

Clearly, the optimistic promise of a utopian life in America made by the Massachusetts Bay Company barely four decades before Goffe's time in Hadley turned out to be false.

How Anglos Responded to
the Indians' Resistance

The colonists' standard view of land originated before Goffe's day and continued long after. It emphasized the progress of civilization that Anglos would bring about. Settlers improved barren land and thus felt they deserved it more than did the roaming natives. John Winthrop in 1630 and later apologists used the legal idea of *vacuum domicilium*, "an empty dwelling place," to justify their taking of Indian land. It was *terra nullius*, "earth that belonged to no one," terrain full of potential that the first inhabitants had not

Figure 17: "A Design to Represent the Beginning and Completion of an American Farm." Pownall 1761.

improved. God apparently blessed the British appropriation:

> [T]his remote, rocky, barren, bushy, wild-woody wilderness, a receptacle for Lions, Wolves, Bears, Foxes, Rockoones, Bags, Bevers, Otters, and all kind of wild creatures, a place never afforded the Natives better than the flesh of a few wild creatures and parch't Indian corn incht out with Chesnuts and bitter Acorns, now through the mercy of Christ become a second England for fertilness in so short a space that it is indeed the wonder of the world. (Johnson 1654, page 173)

Goffe himself observed nature's bounty perfected by man's art when he journeyed up the Connecticut River Valley and saw forests cut down and fields plowed in narrow medieval strips exactly as in England.

Excuses for property theft endured. An eighteenth-century magazine history of Connecticut quoted contemporary sources as it reported how, soon after the colony's founding, "The settlers of Newhaven being refused a grant of land from the Sachem Quinnipiog, immediately voted themselves to be the *children of God,* and that *the wilderness in the utmost parts of the earth given to them.* This vote became a law for ever after.... This brought on a war, which ended in the Indians being driven back into the wood, and the English kept possession of the country." Appropriation of territory became easier as disease diminished the Natives: "the Gospel was spread into every Indian town, and with it the Small Pox." (History Of Connecticut 1781, page 592)

Similarly, a nineteenth-century eulogy of "the first British colonists" said, "A vast and unknown continent, peopled by the ferocious and treacherous Indian, lay before them, and behind them rolled the stormy Atlantic. With hearts as heroic as ever beat within human breasts, these unknown heroes turn their faces toward the setting sun, and commence that glorious march of civilization westward, which is the proudest achievement of our race – nay, I might say with truth, of the human race. The savage is forced back; the forest is cleared; the log hut is reared; the soil is tilled; the crop is sown; the first settlement is planted." (Deverell 1878, page 3)

The Result of English-Indian
Tension in Hadley

During King Philip's War in the 1670s, Hadley had special reason to be nervous. It lay on the north-south route for both newcomers and Indians. The Bloody Brook Massacre in 1673 involved 76 Deerfield men headed with their grain to the mill in North Hadley. Other assaults kept the village agitated. In 1676

Figure 18: Commemorative plaque at North Hadley on east side of route 47.

alone, men in the Hockanum section who had relaxed their vigilance and hiked about on Mount Holyoke were attacked (1 April); massive fires in Hatfield summoned volunteers from Hadley to cross the river and combat raiders (30 May); according to some sources, the Indian offensive that the mysterious Angel thwarted took place on 12 June. Those killings foreshadowed the burning of the mill by Natives in 1677.

Figure 19: Boulder, mill, falls and Lake Warner at North Hadley on east side of route 47.

Figure 20: Detail from Seller 1675.

Stylishly garbed militiamen in Goffe's time defend Hadley from the naked aggressors. Seller was Charles II's official "hydrographer." His pioneering map perhaps highlighted the benefits of a treaty with the Dutch in 1674. When Yale University made a facsimile of it in 1973, an editor surmised that this particular scene referred to Goffe's exploit. As we will see, such exact knowledge by a royalist in London of an otherwise unknown exploit in the New World seems impossible.

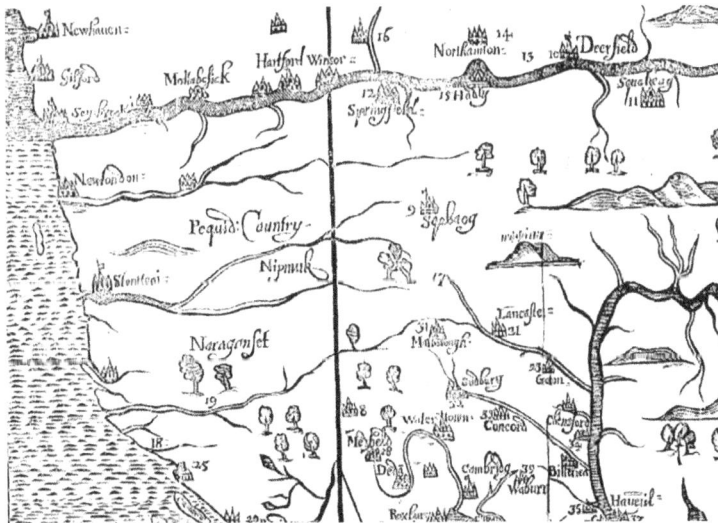

Figure 21: "A Map of New-England." Hubbard 1677A, before page 1.

Hubbard apparently had not seen Seller's map because he claimed his was "the first that ever was here cut." Oriented with north to the right, it located towns that endured raids. No attack on Hadley appeared. He does describe the slaughter of Captain Lathrop's men on the way from Deerfield to Hadley on 8 September 1675. (42) With the bias of his day, Hubbard called native warriors, "the children of the Devill, full of all lechery and malice." (42)

The Long-Lasting Enmity Between
Settlers and Natives

Regrettably, Indians who frustrated the English community's holy tasks of conversion and making a wilderness bloom annoyed Americans until, roughly, the end of the nineteenth century. The few happy instances of a cordial Thanksgiving with Wampanoags in Massachusetts or of a kindly Pocahontas rescuing John Smith in Virginia or of the friendship between the Yamacraw chief Tomochichi and James Oglethorpe in Savannah or of William Penn and original peoples in Pennsylvania were not the memories Goffe and his heirs preserved. In New England, relative peace reigned between the Pequot War of the 1630s and King Philip's War forty years later. In the eighteenth century, the French-Indian Wars and then the uncountable fights as land hungry Americans pursued their manifest destiny and moved westward throughout the 1800s caused bitterness that forbid all but a tiny group of Americans to sympathize with Indians.

When Hutchinson appeared in print, Benjamin Trumbull represented Puritan fears. They explained why Goffe's exploit, once announced, quickly caught the public's attention.

As the Indians had lived promiscuously with the English, in all parts of the country, they were generally as well acquainted with their dwellings, field, and places of worship, as themselves.... This enabled the enemy, not only in small sku[l]king parties, but in great bodies, to make their approaches undiscovered... Notwithstanding every precaution, they continued plundering, burning, killing, and captivating, in one place or another, and kept the whole country in continual fear and alarm. There was no safety to man, woman, nor child; to him who went out, nor to him who came in. Whether they were awake or asleep, whether they journeyed, labored, or worshipped, they were in continual jeopardy. (Trumbull 1797, 1.349)

The negative view of the original inhabitants that outlasted Goffe's era made the Angel story a vital part of the overarching American narrative about a chosen people who defeated danger. Eyewitnesses to Indian cruelty reveled in gory particulars. Benjamin Church, who led troops during King Philip's War, treated his readers to a Grand Guignol vision of butchery at Deerfield in 1703/4 and augmented it with other examples.

Another instance was, of a straggling soldier, who was found at Casco, exposed in a shameful and barbarous manner. His body being staked up, his head cut off, and a hog's head set in the room [in its place]; his body ripped up, and his heart and his inwards taken out, and private members cut off, and hung with belts of their own, the inwards at one side of the body, and his privates at the other, in scorn and derision of the English soldiers. (Church 1716, page 244)

For those Puritans who thought they had escaped from the punishment of Charles II, such mutilation and social disgrace by other enemies must have caused profound agitation.

During the nineteenth century, the popular press continued to print inflammatory material about the ravenous Indians who misbehaved during colonial times. Frequently, Victorian authors presented such narratives as moral lessons. Joshua Leavitt justified his 1833 retelling of Reverend John Williams' tribulations after the 1704 Deerfield Raid:

We have now for so long a time enjoyed the security and happiness of our quiet homes, that we can form little idea of the anxiety and fear which those felt, who were continually exposed to the cruel violence of the cruel savage; and perhaps a review of some of the sufferings which our fathers endured before these blessings were secured to us, will excite our gratitude to God, while we learn to sympathise with the sorrows of our fellow men. (Leavitt 1833, page 6)

Like most special pleadings, these clichéd fantasies of Trumbull and Leavitt pleased already convinced partisans rather than truth seekers. Leavitt misdated the Deerfield Raid. More peculiarly, although he was a prominent Abolitionist and defended Africans who took over the slave ship Amistad in 1839, he showed no sympathy for Native Americans.

Figure 22: Anonymous woodcut (c. 1787): Iroquois about to enslave or kill prisoners.

Journalists employed violent images to sell their publications. The depictions of not-quite-conquered original inhabitants made audiences shiver in something of the same way that modern film viewers recoil from sadistic killers with chain saws or hockey masks.

Figure 23: Another anonymous scene from the French and Indian War warned that the virtues of white men, women and children were useless against the Natives' tomahawks and torches.

Figure 24: Illustration for Plummer 1838, frontpiece.

A similar sad scene portrayed white settlers as victims. It highlighted the burning of the only white male (left). Victorians were convinced that the Christian world had progressed beyond such cruelties. Perhaps the broken tree and the palm-like foliage on the left (the sinister side) of the woodcut connote fallen humans in a ruined garden. The hope of civilization, symbolized on the right by the tidy home and sturdy storage building, thus perilously balances the threat of reversion to savagery.

To make sense of the many horrors, Augusta Berard echoed Leavitt by extracting a moral:

> The details of Indian warfare need not be dwelt upon. They are very horrible: but it is useful sometimes to think of the sufferings of others; and mothers in the pleasant homes of Providence, Springfield, Deerfield, and Hadley, may do well to remember the "heavy hours" of the New England women of a former generation. (Berard 1855, page 30)

Any writers who looked beyond the merely sensational must have known that Indians were often the targets of genocide; in the Anglo mind, however, they deserved extinction. The first two decades of New England relations did not follow any wholesale pattern of conflict or compliance. Yet once hostilities erupted in the Pequot War of the 1630s, the latent ferocity of both sides took over. A contemporary booklet gleefully described the slaughter of 700 Pequot Indians by Captains Mason and Underhill at Mystic, Connecticut, on 26 May 1637. (Vincent 1637) With biblical precedents in mind, the whites felt they were waging a holy war and thus any ideas of mercy did not bind them.

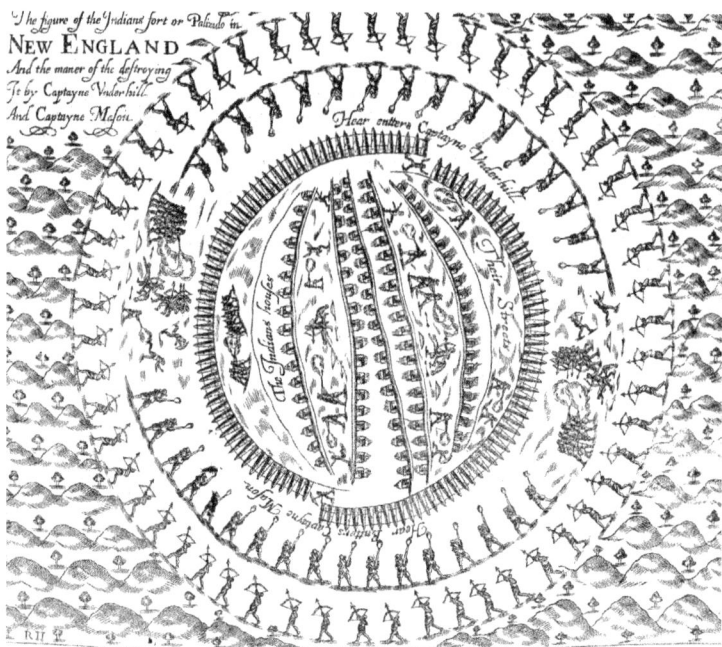

Figure 25: "A Figure of the Indian Fort, or Palizado." Underhill 1638, frontpiece.

A contemporary account of the Mystic massacre contained this woodcut. It is both a realistic sketch and a picture of the American dream of finally being besiegers and despoilers. Ironically, it also predicted future atrocities. Instead of merely illustrating one decisive slaughter, it implied a cycle of alternating victors: as the whites within the palisade exterminate villagers and other whites fire from outside, braves in the outermost circle prepare to discharge their arrows. Statistically, there were fewer conflicts from this time until Philip rose up in Goffe's day; psychologically, the specter of obstinate, recalcitrant, unpredictable natives remained.

Two centuries after this bloodbath, the American ideas of Natives' false religion and their *vacuum domicilium* had so percolated into popular lore that a historical novel began by alluding to "the famous pursuit and slaughter of the brave savages called the Pequods, who in 1637 perished almost to a man, miserably in a wide swamp" near Fairfield, Connecticut. The author restated deep convictions of the immigrants concerning faith and unimproved land. His words tried to ease Victorian consciences about extermination: "No doubt those stern puritans thought they were doing God service in slaying with the sword these 'red heathen savages,' who professed to worship Manitou, the Great Spirit"; a very few Indians remain, but they may in the future learn how to farm:

> Let us hope … that as when the woodman prostrates with his keen axe a forest of the native pines, there springs up from the cleared soil in healthful luxuriance, a grove of sturdy oaks, so a better as well as a mightier people, may increase and multiply, until their contented industry has made one broad smiling garden, of those fields, once the hunting-grounds of the untutored savage, who moulders beneath them, and perished that we might flourish. (Sterling 1848, pages 3-4)

The following two illustrations show how Americans in the growing nation eagerly consumed violent stories from their past. Two formulas governed these Victorian narratives: either the noble white ancestors suffered, or they escaped harm at the hands of brutal Natives. Both narrative patterns supported the Angel legend.

Figure 26: Connecticut 1855, front cover

The motto on the state shield means, "The person who has crossed over will flourish." To illustrate the sentiment, three neatly tied vines clinging to stakes promise a bountiful harvest for those who improve the land. But Pequot warriors, imaged as roving hunter-gatherers, prepare to attack a pious family on its way to church. Note the wife embracing a Bible. The accompanying article noted that in one massacre of Indians, "Fearful was the vengeance inflicted upon the bloody heathen," "the destruction of whom was justified by quotation from Holy Writ."

Figure 27: Chapin, "The Ambush." Ambush 1853, page 273 (front cover).

The Angel story confirmed the slanted anthropology pictured here. Hadley's productive and orthodox farmers exemplified an evolved community. It nearly perished at the hands of roaming marauders driven by atavistic motives of revenge or ransom. The antagonism between those who cut down the profitless forest or plowed open land and those who merely wandered through them was playing out in the day of this article. Our far west saw "nesters" fence in their property and impede cattlemen, who sought open range. Nevertheless, both these white groups benefited society; few contemporaries of Goffe could find any reason for Native Americans to live.

The three-page article accompanying Chapin's picture of "The Ambush" melodramatically told how in 1703 or 1704 near Worcester, Massachusetts, these "fierce Indians," "mad for vengeance and thirsting for blood," spied the loving husband going to cut trees in the forest and leaving behind his defenseless wife ("a woman of deep Christian feeling") and five children. The "infuriated savages" chased him down, scalped him and, later, his wife. They transported the children to Canada, where two of them accepted adoption, never to return to the "little Arcadia in the heart of the wilderness." The didactic point of the story was to remind readers "of those early scenes in the daily experiences of our forefathers, to which we can never recur too frequently." (Ambush 1853, page 273, front cover) In addition, John Barber in 1839 offered the Sargeant incident to characterize Worcester. (Barber 1839, pages 618-19) The Sargeant murders furthered the assumption of the Angel audiences from his day onward that hidden foes intended to despoil decent settlers who needed protection.

Goffe's exploit commanded attention for so many years because it appealed to later audiences who were convinced that, as General Benjamin Lincoln said, "the Indian nations will never be civilized. . . . Nature forbids civilized and uncivilized people possessing the same territory." Lincoln's rueful prediction was that the Indians, with their poverty-stricken vocabulary, love of ease and habit of overhunting, would retreat northward and "cease to be a people." (Lincoln 1795) His relatively compassionate view, however, was wrong; the Natives survived and goaded nineteenth century whites to preserve old fears of rebellion and dreams of a hero who could protect "civilization."

The mixture of aversion and yearning appeared so often that it became the standard. One example may represent others: in *The American Ladies' Magazine* of 1836, a poet followed Stiles' account when describing "The ruthless red man of the forest haunts" who, lusting for scalps and women, terrified the Hadley congregation as it fasted and prayed that "The Christian God give succor." Sure enough, a mysterious "Champion or Seer" like Moses or Jephtha appeared to save them. (The Angel of Hadley 1836)

The Beginning of the
Angel Legend

If we keep in our minds these concerns of the Puritans -- sin, false faiths, monarchy and Indians -- then we can see how the Angel of Hadley incident would have satisfied the chosen community's hunger for some figure to defend it against butchery by outsiders and proclaim its special place in a divine plan. However, Puritans did not record the Angel story as we know it.

How did the hero tale begin? Increase Mather in 1674/1676 supplied the first hint:

> Wherefore *September* 1[, 1675], the *Indians* set upon *Deerfield* (alias *Pacomtuck*) and killed one man, and laid most of the Houses in that new hopeful Plantation in ruinous heaps. That which added solemnity and awfulness to that desolation is, that it happened on the very day when one of the Churches in *Boston* were seeking the face of God by Fasting and Prayer before him. Also that very day the Church in *Hadly* was before the Lord in the same way, but were driven from the Holy Service they were attending by a most sudden and violent *Alarm*, which routed them the whole day after. So that we may humbly complain, as sometimes the Church did, *How long hast thou smoaked*

against עשנת [*ashant*, "ignored, been angry at." Miscopied from the Hebrew of Psalm 74.1] *the Prayers of thy People?* (Mather 1674 /1676, pages 7-8. I quote from the London edition)

From this cryptic mention of some "*Alarm*," the Angel myth grew. Perhaps Mather meant to emphasize that a just God controls history and punishes sinners with catastrophes such as invasion. He may allude to the book of Judges. It supported a three-part cycle for Hebrew history: first, decent behavior and prosperity; then, degeneration into apostasy and invasion; next, repentance and the arrival of a "judge," or military deliverer. The biblical book listed twelve heroes who, in greater or smaller exploits, overcame Canaanite enemies. Mather no doubt wondered why his flock was so vexed and no savior arrived. Cooper later linked the cyclical pattern of Judges with Indian depredation in *Wept of Wish-ton-Wish*. The zealous preacher, "had chosen for his text on that day [of an Indian attack], a passage from the book of Judges: 'And the children of Israel did evil in the sight of the Lord; and the Lord delivered them into the hands of Midian seven years.'" (Cooper 1829. Mohawk edition, chapter 22, page 278)

Historians can verify the Deerfield assault mentioned by Mather. The letter that concluded his notice, no doubt from John Russell, mentioned many Indian encounters – but no notice of an attack, no rescue or no mysterious defender in Hadley.

What is Unusual about
Mather's Vagueness?

With almost masochistic precision, Goffe's contemporaries eagerly noted attacks. During June 1675, Indians assaulted Swansea twice (20 and 24), Taunton (27) and Old Rehoboth (30); during July, Middleboro and Dartmouth (9) and Mendon (14); during August, captains Hutchinson and Wheeler at Brookfield (2), Lancaster (22), captains Lathrop and Beers in the Whately Swamp (25) and Springfield (30); during September, Deerfield (1), Springfield (2), Beers killed at Northfield (4), Topsham, Maine (5), Deerfield (12), Lathrop killed at Bloody Brook (18) and Northampton (28). Mather's *Brief History*, the longest and most eloquent recital of Native atrocities, obliquely mentioned some happening in "Hadly." Other reports supplied copious details about attacks on other New England towns, barbarous treatment of whites, lists of casualties and, occasionally, small victories. For example, in 1677, William Hubbard offered a resume of recent local battles. However, neither he nor the compilers listed below mentioned any commotion at places closer than Deerfield, Northampton or Springfield. (Hubbard 1677)

Similarly, at the time of Goffe's alleged rescue, the Massachusetts Bay Council, which also kept careful track of incursions, quickly responded to kidnappings from Hadley's neighbor.

At a Council held at Boston the 22d. of August 1678: Whereas Benjamin Wait and Stephen Jennings of Hadley on the 24ᵗʰ. Of October last 1677. Were appointed and ordered by the honoured Govenour John Leveret Esq. To take their journey to Canada in order to their procuring the several English captives that were taken by the Indians from Hatfield on the 19ᵗʰ. of September last.

To compensate the redeemed captives, the Council sent £13 6s plus "three yards and half of Kersey [cloth]" to "Mr. *John Russel* Minister of Hadley and to Mr. *Solomon Stoddard* Minister of North-Hampton." (At A Council 1678) Yet the ever-vigilant state recorded no disorder at Hadley.

The Search for a Savior

Admittedly, the argument from silence has little validity in historical discussions. If the Angel had saved Hadley at this time, there obviously would have been no captives for the Council to buy back. Still, the full Angel anecdote as we have it now would have satisfied a question that goaded all settlers: when will God fortify someone to save us from destruction? The desire to change from victim to victor caused people to analyze every report. They sought any hint that God's wrath against them was diminishing. They could not ignore afflictions that appeared too plainly, too often and too painfully. Books and pamphlets from Goffe's time promised specific information about the varied raids so audiences could look at particular acts and perhaps discern a larger plan unfolding. The subtitle of one work by Nathaniel Saltonstall indicated the marketing strategy used to sell publications to anxious settlers at home and relatives back in England: *A New and Further Narrative of the State of New-England; Being a Continued Account of the Bloudy Indian-War, from March till August, 1676. Giving a Perfect Relation of the Several Devastations, Engagements, and Transactions There: as also the Great Successes Lately Obtained Against the Barbarous Indians … Together with a Catalogue of the Losses in the Whole, Sustaining on Either Side Since the Said War Began, as Near as can be Collected* (Saltonstall 1676 A, title page).

In a second work from 1676, Saltonstall recorded the killing of Captain Beers and fifty-five troops who had left Hadley to aid the beleaguered Deerfield community. His successor, Captain Moseley, rescued one of the wounded whites, carrying him nineteen miles to safety: "and now this Man is well again and in good health." (Saltonstall 1676, page 14) If Moseley had not appeared, the young man might have suffered unspeakable agonies. A third of Saltonstall's booklets avidly reckoned up the consequences of defeat by the Indians:

> Men, Women and Children ... have been destroyed with exquisite Torments and most inhumane barbarities, the Heathen rarely giving Quarter to those that they take, but if they were Women, first forced them to satisfie their filthy lusts, and then murthered them, either cutting off the head, ripping open the Belly, or sculping the head of skin and hair, and hanging them up as Trophies; wearing mens fingers as bracelets about their Necks, and stripes of their skins which they dresse for Belts: They knockt one Youth of the Head, and laying him face down, they flesd (or skulp'd) his head of skin and hair.

This young man survived, as had Captain Moseley's soldier, and introduced a favorite motif of atrocity stories. Deity superintended all human activities and occasionally hinted at a good outcome in the future: "I think it is high time to conclude, with hearty thanks to Almighty God for our late successes against this bloody Enemy ... we have grounds to hope, that their fury is much quasht and abated, so that (if our sins obstruct not so greate a blessing) we may shortly once again see peace and safety restored to our (lately disconsolate) habitations in this wilderness." (Saltonstall 1676 B, page 14)

Contemporaries desperately looked for a change in power relations with the Native Americans; they sought a liberator. News reports employed the usual theological explanation for the war: directed by God, it punished an erring faith group. Only a wholesale renovation of right belief could rescue congregations from his iron rod. The sign that the Deity has found repentance in their hearts will be the arrival of a champion who, like the biblical Joshua or Samson, defeats infidels. Consequently, observers throughout New England sought and publicized every skirmish to confirm that the Almighty had relented. Benjamin Tompson meditated on "the Dolefull *tidings* of New Massacres, Slaughters and *Devastations* committed by the *Brutish Heathens*" and "the savage Cruelties of a bloody (and sometimes despicable) Enemy" in 1676. Ordinary humans cannot withstand these attackers, "unless our God (whose tender mercies are ever of his works) in compassion to the English Nation in this Wildernesse, wonderfully appear for our deliverance." Infrequently, the Deity rescued someone. Eight Indians captured "some Christians going to a Meeting at Springfield." Providentially, "Major Savage at Hadly" rushed to their aid, chased them off and "the woman revived," although "the bloody Villains for the present escaped deserved vengeance." Contemporaries read such small acts as God's reassurance that the one deliverer typified others to come. (Thomson 1676, 1; 6) Audiences fervently sought other examples of salvation.

A

NARRATIVE

OF THE

CAPTIVITY, SUFFERINGS AND REMOVES

OF

Mrs. *Mary Rowlandson,*

Who was taken Prifoner by the INDIANS with feveral others, and treated in the moft barbarous and cruel Manner by thofe vile Savages : With many other remarkable Events during her TRAVELS.

Written by her own Hand, for her private Ufe, and now made public at the earneft Defire of fome Friends, and for the Benefit of the afflicted.

BOSTON

Printed and Sold at JOHN BOYLE's Printing-Office, next Door to the *Three Doves* in Marlborough-Street. 1773.

Figure 28: The Title Page of the tenth edition (1773) testifies to the continuing appeal of Rowlandson's Narrative. She emphasized two of the community's ideas. First, God sends us tribulation, either to punish us or to test us so we can show our worthiness; also, Catholics and Indians are foes.

"I only am escaped"(Job 1:15) -
Some Settlers who
Evaded Indian Abuse

A few months before Hadley's supposed reprieve, Mary Rowlandson (c. 1637-1711) of Lancaster survived four months of abduction by "Narrhagannsetts" (from 1 February 1675/1676). Her 1682 memoir began the first American literary genre, the captivity narrative. Eastern Indians kidnapped settlers to ransom, to adopt into villages emptied by white man's diseases, to torture or to trade with other tribes. They especially prized and usually did not abuse Anglo females age seven to fifteen. Many girls chose to remain with their new Indian families, a worry to settlers. During Mary's detention, she used Native American words and once earned a knife in payment for her labor, proofs that whites and Indians had evolved mechanisms to interact and were not so foreign as many of the accounts cited above implied. Covertly, the *Narrative* insists that her captors had not contaminated her and she could reenter Lancaster.

A second captivity account makes even more curious Mather's reticence about the salvation later attributed to Goffe. A raiding party that included Bampico, a Native American who had lived with the Rowlandson family in Lancaster, kidnapped Hannah Emerson Duston (1657-1737) from Haverhill on 15 March 1697. Forced to watch as her captors dashed out the brains of her newborn daughter against a tree and then hurried north for fifteen days, Duston finally revenged herself. With the help of another woman and a teenage fellow prisoner, she waited until the Indians slept, seized tomahawks, murdered and scalped them. After Mary returned to Haverhill, the state paid her a bounty for the scalps.

Duston's triumph satisfied a powerful need in her harassed community. No matter whether God was punishing them by means of the Indian incursions or whether he was testing their faith, people felt helpless. Duston's exploit was widely reported, encouraging the instinctive hunger for protection from the natives and, if compromised, for escape and revenge. Notable authors retold her story: Cotton Mather; Samuel Sewall; John Marshall; Timothy Dwight; John Greenleaf Whittier; Henry David Thoreau; and Nathaniel Hawthorne. A century after her ordeal, Haverhill erected a statue of her, the first monument to a woman in the United States.

The following three illustrations of Duston's revenge catered to American audiences. Set in the dark forest, that impediment to agriculture, during a gothic night, the captives reversed roles and validated a gender belief (one white woman is better than any number of Indians). Duston's act did not violate the do not kill commandment because self-defense and justice required it.

Figure 29: "Hannah Duston's Escape from Contoocook Island, New Hampshire (now known as Dustin Island) on the night of March 29th-30th, 1697. The two-acre island is at the junction of the Merrimack and Contoocook Rivers north of Concord. Samuel Leonardson, the fourteen-year-old English boy, is also seen in the illustration assisting in the killing of the Indians." Hannah Duston No Date

Figure 30: "Hannah Duston." Stearns 1847.

This, the earliest painting of the executions, took liberties with fact by picturing three women instead of two and by omitting the boy. Grim though the act was, the strong diagonal axis and the symmetrical poses of the women convey dignified energy. Obviously, the narrative will end successfully: the woman on the right will save her endangered companion in the middle.

Figure 31: "Dustin, Neff, and Leonardson." Caverly 1875, page 28.

Duston, Mary Neff (1646-1720) and the English lad Leonardson (c. 1683-?) dispatch their guards in front of stereotypical wigwams. Although most Protestant Bibles eliminated the Apocrypha, the book of Judith told a similar story. The virtuous widow in a besieged Hebrew city visited the enemy general in his tent at night and decapitated him, effectively ending the attack. The American frontier carried on this tradition of revenge. (Tom Quick 1904)

Like these contemporary accounts of Rowlandson and Duston, John Williams' (1664-1729) *The Redeemed Captive Returning to Zion* (1706/1707), frequently reprinted, detailed the 1704 sacking of Deerfield by Indians, forced march to Canada and repatriation of some villagers.

Titus Strong's *The Deerfield Captive* (1832) a retelling of Williams' ordeal, inculcated vigilance against foes for students living more than a century after Goffe and the Deerfield raid.

Figure 32: Attack on Ensign John Sheldon's house, the "Indian House," on 29 February 1703/4 at Deerfield. Leavitt 1833, frontpiece. Also in Johnson 1897, page 29.

Martyrdom had been a staple of Christian behavior since New Testament times. Williams' audience confronted what seemed in his day to be a collision of two irreconcilable systems. His group had quarreled equally with Anglo-Catholic monarchs and other Protestant sects with little thought of compromise. One late nineteenth-century account reminded readers, "Whenever any serious disagreement arose the dissentients usually withdrew and founded a new settlement... Hadley was the outcome of church quarrels in Hartford and Wethersfield." (Hadley's Many Memories 1887, page 11) Surrounded everywhere by Indians, settlers' relations with them constantly wavered between business contracts and horrific conflict.

Pictures such as these appealed to xenophobes living long after Goffe's time. Titus Strong's anti-Indian prejudice soon would join anti-Catholic bigotry that formed the Loyal Orange Association and the Know Nothing party. Resentment of all foreigners in the next decades of the nineteenth century, especially the Irish, the Poles and the Italians, became normative. In fields as varied as politics and boxing, long-time Americans sought one of their own to conquer upstart newcomers.

Figure 33: Braves ambush one of two groups of unwary whites. 1. On 18 September 1675, Captain Lathrop's young soldiers on their way from Deerfield to North Hadley with grain for the mill died at Bloody Brook. The inexperienced troopers negligently piled their weapons on the wagons and gathered grapes. From original company of 80, "all, but seven or eight, fell in the battle." 2. In 1676, at the falls between Greenfield and Montague, "Capt. Turner and thirty seven men were killed, but the Indians suffered a much greater loss." (Strong 1832, page 20)

Hutchinson's Note
about the Angel

After Mather's enigmatic remark concerning some alarm in Hadley, the atypical silence lasted for nearly a century. According to Hoyt, "The story of the judges [in Hadley] was first given to the world in 1764, by governor Hutchinson, who obtained it from manuscripts found among the papers of the Mather family of Boston; by whom they are supposed to have been procured from the descendants of Mr. Russel [sic]. Its development during the lives of the actors in the scene, would have exposed them to imminent danger, and perhaps cost them their lives." (Hoyt 1824, pages 84-85) Here is Hutchinson's first notice.

> September the 1st, Hadley was attacked upon a fast day, while the people were at church, which broke up the service, and obliged them to spend the day in a very different exercise. (Hutchinson 1765, 1.218)

Once again, we read without being enlightened. Hutchinson, a former royal lieutenant governor, had access to Goffe's papers. These crucial documents unfortunately disappeared when anti-Tory mobs ransacked his home in 1765. Hutchinson described only some sort of challenge and some sort of obscure response: "a very different exercise." Meaning what?

Hutchinson's third volume, published posthumously in 1828, said in a footnote:

> The town of Hadley was alarmed by the Indians in 1675, in the time of publick worship, and the people were in the utmost confusion. Suddenly, a grave elderly person appeared in the midst of them. In his mien and dress he differed from the rest of the people. He not only encouraged them to defend themselves; but put himself at their head, rallied, instructed and led them on to encounter the enemy, who by this means were repulsed. As suddenly, the deliverer of Hadley disappeared. The people were left in consternation utterly unable to account for this strange phoenomenon. It is not probable that they were ever able to explain it. If Goffe had then been discovered, it must have come to the knowledge of those persons, who declare by their letters that they never knew what became of him. (Hutchinson's footnote on 1.215, quoted in Stiles 1794, page 29)

Although Hutchinson gave place and date to the episode, he could find no evidence of the tradition in Hadley itself. Yet his mention of the danger to those who concealed Goffe began to explain why the story appeared so long after the supposed event. Although he disapproved of both the American and French revolutions, he seemed sympathetic to the hunted Puritan, but only as an object lesson against insurrection. Hutchinson's contemporary Mark Noble also saw Goffe's long exile as a just but heartrending punishment for rebellion that "ought to be a lesson written in brass, to deter men from enormous vices." (Noble 1798, page 256)

New England of the late eighteenth century was receptive to this anecdote of concealed heroism. True or not, it needed to be invented. The region still had strong anti-monarchial and anti-Indian sentiments. Hounded by the king's detectives until he died, the regicide as described by Hutchinson still triumphed: he frustrated the Stuarts, who wished to nullify Puritan civic and spiritual power. Goffe prefigured the ideology that energized our own American Revolution.

Another Footnote
Concerning the Angel

A curious footnote in a poem dedicated to the regicides implied that some people knew the rescue tale 30 years before Hutchinson's 1828 note appeared publicly. In stilted language, Philagathos ("Lover of the Good"), a pen name for Ezra Stiles, President of Yale, said about Goffe's and Whalley's hiding at parson Russell's:

> The pair colleague remain sequester'd still,
>> Nor see of Adam's race nor e'er are seen
> Save when they succor the assaulted vill, [village]
>> Or, with familiars clos'd for prayer convene.

The author explained the reference in line three with this note:

> The following anecdote is traditional in Hadley: The settlement there, being attacked by Indians, in 1675, during public worship, were put in consternation and entirely routed.
>
> Immediately a venerable old personage appeared, reconnoitered the people, and led them on to victory. Their angelic preserver, as suddenly, disappeared, and the seemingly supernatural phaenomenon could never be explained. (Stiles 1793, page 22)

Stiles' Elaboration
of the Angel Incident

So far, Mather, Hutchinson and Philagathos disappoint us. We want the full operatic tale. Ezra Stiles, writing under his own name in 1794, finally articulated it:

They [Goffe and Whalley] came to Hadley October 1664... Though told with some variation in some parts of New-England, the true story of the Angel is this: -- During their abode in Hadley, the famous and most memorable Indian war that ever was in New-England, called Philip's War, took place ... and Hadley ... [was] ... then an exposed frontier. That pious congregation were observing a Fast at Hadley on the occasion of this war: and being at public worship in the meeting-house there on a Fast day, September 1, 1675, were suddenly surrounded and surprized by a body of Indians. It was the usage in the frontier towns ... for a select number of the congregation to go armed to public worship. It was so in Hadley at this time. The people immediately took to their arms, but were thrown into great consternation and confusion. Had Hadley been taken, the discovery of the Judges had been inevitable. Suddenly, and in the midst of the people there appeared a man of very venerable aspect, and different from the inhabitants in his apparel, who took the command, arranged, and ordered them in the best military manner, and under his direction they repelled and routed the Indians, and the town was saved. He immediately vanished, and the inhabitants could not account for the phoenomenon, but by considering that person as an Angel sent of God upon that special occasion for their deliverance. Nor did they know or conceive otherwise till fifteen or twenty years after, when it at length became known at Hadley that the two judges had been secreted there; which probably they did not know till after Mr. Russel's death, in 1692.... The mystery was unriddled after the revolution, when it became not so very dangerous to have it known that the Judges had received an asylum here.... The Angel was certainly General Goffe, for Whalley was superannuated in 1675. (Stiles 1794, pages 109-10)

Stiles claimed he was reproducing both Hutchinson's now-lost journal and local traditions he had gathered at Hadley during his visit in 1793. As a Whig, he sought to defuse Mather's accusation of sin and punishment as well as Hutchinson's conservative disapproval of revolt. Thus Stiles emphasized the providential salvation of an imperiled group of the faithful. Puritans typically saw history as a series of predictions and fulfillments, of types and antitypes. Type denoted any person, act or word that happened and simultaneously pointed to a more important restatement (the antitype) in the future. Jonah belched up from the belly of the great fish supplied the type; its fulfillment was Jesus bursting from his tomb or from Hell. So, too, in Stiles' mind, Goffe gave historical legitimacy to yet another rebellion against London. Reformation Protestants had used consciously old-fashioned language when they translated their Bibles so their new church would seem to be as old as the Catholics'. In the same way, apologists like Stiles used exemplars from the respected past to glorify their current uprising against George III.

Also, Stiles tried to distract attention from the shocking news that French zealots had recently guillotined Louis XVI. Like Milton in the previous century, he distinguished between a lawful king and a tyrant, thereby reserving sympathy for Goffe, not a monarch. Stiles protected the character of the Hadley townspeople who thought an angel had visited them by furnishing the reason that no one of them publicized the miracle. All would have suffered if their brave concealment had been revealed to the vindictive pursuivants Kirk and Kellond.

Unfortunately, those modern researchers who want to use Stiles' account as proof of the Angel's legitimacy must read it with extreme skepticism. His version of several events in New Haven contradicted facts later gained from manuscripts made public after his *History of Three of the Judges*. (Dexter 1876) A contemporary of Stiles, Charles William Janson, commented about the *History*, "A work more eccentric I never saw. A variety of subjects ... are there jumbled together, interspersed with old women's tales, in the most trite and barren language; and spun out by an insufferable tautology to three hundred and fifty-seven pages." (Janson 1807, Carl S. Driver edition, page 55) Trowbridge 1877 tried to defend Stiles' reliability, but he did not restore confidence among most readers. Lemuel Aiken Welles raised another caution about Stiles' accuracy. The latter "collected many traditions and anecdotes about the regicides in Connecticut. Some of these could not have happened and some are stock stories of fugitives...That the regicides were at one time in Guilford rests only on traditions recorded by President Stiles over a century after their deaths." (Welles 1935, page 31) Rollin G. Osterweis agreed that Stiles might be read for pleasure, not precision. (Osterweis 1953)

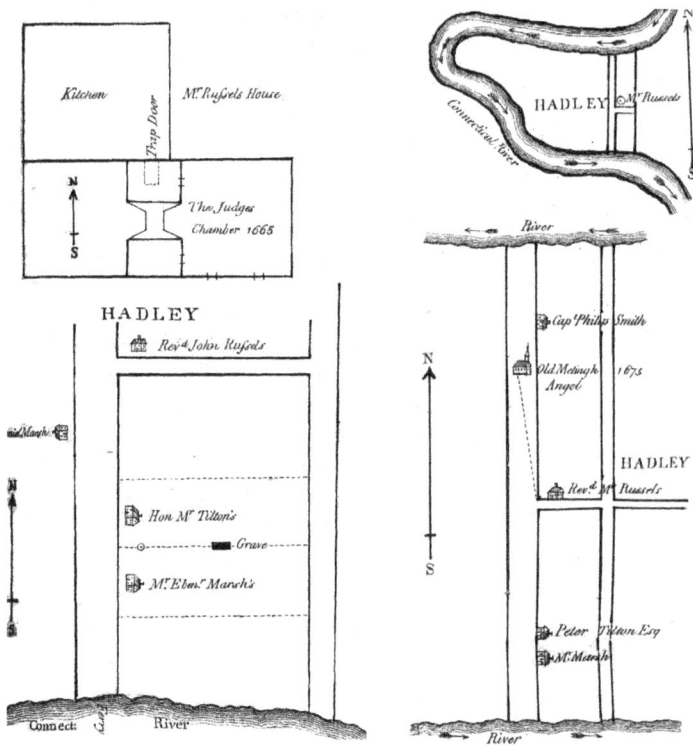

Figure 34: Hadley as pictured in Stiles 1794, facing pages 115; 202.

Note closeness of the Smith, John Russell, Peter Tilton and Ebenezer Marsh houses. A letter quoted by Stiles and Judd 1863, 211, says Goffe hid at Russell's, Tilton's and Smith's. Judd gives the latter name as "Lieut. Samuel Smith."

Dwight's Continuation
of the Legend

Another Yale President, Timothy Dwight, further described the rescue in 1805.

The following story has been traditionally conveyed down among the inhabitants of Hadley.

In the course of Philip's war, which involved almost all the Indian tribes in New-England, and among others those in the neighbourhood of this town, the inhabitants thought it proper to observe the 1st of September, 1675, as a day of fasting and prayer. While they were in the church, and employed in their worship, they were surprised by a band of savages. The people instantly betook themselves to their arms, which, according to the custom of the times, they had carried with them to the church: and, rushing out of the house, attacked their invaders. The panic, under which they began the conflict, was however so great, and their number was so disproportioned to that of their enemies, that they fought doubtfully at first, and in a short time began evidently to give way. At this moment, an ancient man with hoary locks, of a most venerable and dignified aspect, and in a dress widely differing from that of the inhabitants, appeared suddenly at their head; and with a firm voice, and an example of undaunted resolution, reanimated their spirits, led them again to the conflict, and totally routed the savages. When the battle was ended, the stranger disappeared; and no person knew whence he had come, or whither he had gone. The relief was so timely, so sudden, so unexpected, and so providential; the appearance, and the retreat, of him, who furnished it, were so unaccountable; his person was so dignified and commanding, his resolution so superiour, and his interference so decisive; that the inhabitants, without any uncommon exercise of credulity, readily believed him to be an Angel, sent by Heaven for their preservation. Nor was this opinion seriously controverted, until it was discovered, several years afterward, that Goffe and Whalley had been lodged in the house of Mr. Russell. Then it was known, that their deliverer was Goffe: Whalley having become superannuated sometime before the event took place. (Dwight 1821, pages 353-54)

Born in Northampton, Dwight made his fact-gathering journey to Hadley during September 1796. For this Angel tradition, he generally reproduced the written material of Hutchinson and Stiles. However, Dwight added two new details. First, he pictured the champion "with hoary locks," understandable for a man in his 60s. Certainly, the hair harmonized with Goffe's old-fashioned garb, although most everyone wore clothing until it fell apart. Sir Walter Scott apparently inserted his version of the Angel myth into his novel *Peveril* after reading this passage in Dwight.

Second, Dwight saw all the Indians as "savages." Such disparagement echoed the usual denigration of outsiders that most nations employ. By the early nineteenth century, as we have seen, fear of Indians escalated after they sided with the French during the French Indian Wars and with the English during the War of 1812. Dozens of pathetic or horrific accounts of abuse by Indians expanded the earliest American literary genre, the captivity narrative, as introduced by Mary Rowlandson and John Williams. The pattern of surprise assault, capture, tribulations and, sometimes, release furnished the plot for countless other popular narratives. Atrocities became a required ingredient and would have made Goffe's rescue even more appealing: every now and then, a champion could protect homes and families against barbarians.

Facts about Goffe
and Suppositions about the Angel

Later artistic metamorphoses appear below, but for now, let us sum up the facts about William Goffe as generally accepted by impartial historians.

- The Puritan Major General, son of a preacher, earned his reputation as a pious military leader. Once he had notably inspired his Roundhead soldiers in 1648 with a stirring political sermon (expanding Proverbs 1:23: "I have called and ye refused") on their need to act against the king.

- Goffe was one of the 1649 regicide judges, allied by marriage with Oliver Cromwell and fellow general Edward Whalley, and, as such, a most wanted man after Charles II regained the throne in 1660.

- Even before the Restoration, Goffe fled England.

- Goffe had a wide network of allies in New England, but Boston, New Haven and Hartford became too dangerous for him because royal agents Thomas Kellond and Thomas Kirk pursued him. According to Charles' order, anyone harboring the judges would be drawn, hung, disemboweled, beheaded and quartered. Also, the monarch offered a reward of £100 for turning in the fugitives.

- Reverend John Russell and Deacon Peter Tilton in the young community of Hadley, strong partisan Puritans, had left Wethersfield, Connecticut, because of doctrinal disagreements. They probably welcomed Goffe in October 1664 and passed him from one safe house to another.

- Although a small town, Hadley had farmers, state functionaries, artisans, traders, servants and visiting soldiers continually milling about. It is possible that Goffe could have remained there incognito. There are precedents. After the Vatican condemned Martin Luther in 1521, his patron Frederick the Wise secreted him for almost a year in Wartburg castle near Weimar; similarly, English Catholics hid in "priests' holes" (concealed chambers in old religionists' homes) during Protestant persecutions, though not for so many years. Robbins 1869 offered a patriotic defense of the villagers' silence about the wanted men in their midst:

> It is certainly a matter of surprise that their secret could have been kept so well. The people of Hadley appear to have been ignorant of their residence among them, and it is probable that very few persons, even among the most intimate associates of their protectors, had any knowledge of their place of concealment…It would seem that not only no one was willing to betray them, but that everyone purposely endeavored not to know where they were. Such tender compassion, and such delicate and even sacred consideration for these hunted exiles, whose greatest crime was a desperate blow at oppression, and who had confidently thrown themselves upon their protection, are among those noble traits in the character of our Fathers, which claim honorable commemoration from their descendants, and should never fail – as, thank God, they seldom have failed – to excite their generous emulation. (Pages 25-26)

I, too, accept the tradition that Goffe spent some of his exile in Hadley.

Now for speculations about the Angel legend.

- 1 September 1675 was said to have been a fast day in Hadley. There is little reason to debate this assertion because no facts affirm or deny it. Yet a possible vigil by the congregation does not validate a simultaneous attack by Natives.

- French and Indian forces – Catholics and idolaters, in the settlers' view – attacked Deerfield on 1 September. All neighboring communities thus were on high alert. Verifiably accurate.

- If the fast took place on another date (19 October 1675 and 12 June 1676 have been suggested), the same logic must apply: pious ritual is separate from a reputed incursion.

- No matter what date we choose for Goffe's exploit, no contemporary historian, no pamphleteer, no diarist, no reporter to the Massachusetts Bay Council or no letter writer mentioned a magical salvation. It would be nearly inconceivable that the community we have described would not immediately have publicized such an apparently divine appearance. Salem and Hadley itself within a few years would soon believe that invisible evils were molesting their citizens by witchcraft; how much more easily would Hadley residents, billeted soldiers or passers-by remark on a visible raid and public rescue?

Bayne 1892 supplied a vigorous explanation:

> This appearance of Goffe has been doubted by some; but when we consider that these men lived in Hadley as a Nihilist would live in Russia, or a 'dynamiter' be hidden in England, with the 'shadowy figure of the executioner ever stalking behind them,' we realize how foolish it would be to make written record of a

rash act of heroism, which might draw the bolt, swift and relentless, to scathe not only the actor but the protector. The writers of Hadley, those most likely to note such an event in letters or diaries, were too much interested in letting the occurrence sink into oblivion before it raised inconvenient curiosity and investigation. (Pages 333-34)

Wilson 1987 made the most cogent case for secrecy by pointing out that contemporary historians like Daniel Gookin was Goffe's friend and Richard Saltonstall the son of a friend. Moreover, the army commanders near Hadley on that date, John Talcott and Benjamin Newberry, were John Russell's brothers-in-law. None of them would have betrayed the old hero.

- Theories such as these by Bayne and Wilson, plausible as they are at first reading, fail to take into account the many non-Puritan witnesses to any rescue. All the other uncommitted merchants, troopers and even townspeople cannot be assumed to have the same self-control against gossip. Soldiers may have arrived too late to witness the defense or not seen the elderly leader. However, to assume such fortunate blindness on the part of outsiders and absolute unanimity of thought among villagers (ever quarrelsome in so many matters) for so long probably romanticizes the power of communal harmony.

Considering these data, I reject the Angel account as a convenient fiction, one that later writers invented and elaborated to further their personal views, not to capture authentic history.

Why do We Still Want the
Angel Story to be True?

Historians have long since abandoned the dream that they can discover objective truth about events. As the ancient Greeks explained, there are two separate ways of processing experience. We may believe something (my constant companion is an invisible, tall white rabbit named Harvey; my grandsons are the world's most appealing youngsters). Those assertions, however compelling to the professor, are private and not necessarily valid for everyone. In contrast, we may know something (the earth moves around the sun; the prefrontal cortex of the brain controls social decisions) and all reasonable people can agree because objective data and replicable experiments uniformly support these affirmations.

Sometimes verifiable reality seems drab and we prefer pleasant inventions. As proud Americans, we want Plymouth Rock and George Washington's cherry tree to be accurate. They supply a visitable place and a useful moral. An Italian proverb says, "Even if not true, it's well expressed." To bond with our community, we often reverse the scientific process by assuming something and then selecting facts to back it up. A few class-conscious readers believe Shakespeare's plays are too sophisticated to have been written by anyone from a village; therefore they amass biographical data about some aristocrat to prove he composed them.

Goffe as hero in Hadley presents us with a difficult decision. His alleged act seems plausible based upon his known personality. He demonstrated by previous deeds in England that he was a pious believer and a capable military man. A man of his era, motivated by fear and *ira bona*, "righteous anger," he exhibited zeal, not empathy or negotiation, when he fought hostile forces according to the biblical idea of holy war.

Goffe's demonstrable virtues may seem dated, but they harmonize with the deed that made Hadley famous. Potential, however, does not guarantee performance. Pride in one's town often leads to slanted logic that extends a famous person's career beyond observable actions. New Haven made the same eager claim for its local legend about the graves of the regicides. Here are the words of a "town-born" defender of the flattering tale that Dexter 1876 had questioned:

> Mr. President: — The paper which has now been read, if permitted to go uncontradicted, will perhaps destroy one of the historical events in the history of the town, or at least convey to the minds of some a doubt respecting the resting place of the renowned regicides. I am constrained therefore to give to the meeting a few thoughts connected with the history, and corroborative of the legend which has for so many years been cherished by our townsmen, and particularly by the town-born. It has, for nearly two hundred years, been most religiously believed that the three regicides were buried in New Haven. (Trowbridge 1877, page 147)

Those of us who want the story of Goffe's rescue to be proven either true or false must accept the impossibility of any universally acceptable decision. His surviving letters from 1662-1679 support neither opinion. The authors who came after him had their own purposes for taking sides and were no better equipped than we are to transport themselves back to Hadley's common in the 1670s to observe whatever did or did not happen. Perhaps the wisest way to maintain Goffe as deliverer is to adopt the habit of biblical scholars. They disagree about details for the earthly careers of Moses, David and Jesus, but they understand that those men transcended video-recorder reality. Each symbolized a group's assumptions and aspirations and therefore communicated spiritual truth. So, too, can we accept Goffe as both a verifiable individual who, say, definitely signed Charles I's death warrant, and, when discussing the Angel incident, an emblem to which later commentators assigned significance according to their current needs. Therefore, we may temporarily ignore the demands of scientific history while we preserve him as an attractive cultural object in the amber of constructed nostalgia.

Figure 35: Goffe rallying Hadley residents No Date

Literary Adaptation of the
Angel Incident by Scott

Many imaginative authors, plus graphic artists and antiquarians, mentioned below, retold the legend. They owed much to the primary records already cited and to Sir Walter Scott, the great historical novelist. He popularized the incident to an enormous audience in his 1822 novel *Peveril of the Peak*. The bewildering narrative involves arrests, imprisonments and pardons. A popish plot to kill Charles II so his Catholic brother can seize the throne plus the love of the children of Peveril and Bridgenorth supply motives to bizarre characters: a half Moorish woman who pretends to be a deaf mute in order to spy, a lustful courtier and an imperiled maiden.

Set in 1678, the following conversation takes place between the elderly Puritan Ralph Bridgenorth and Julian, a young Cavalier, son of the old Cavalier Geoffrey Peveril, who shelters Bridgenorth in Derbyshire. Years ago, says Bridgenorth, he witnessed the Angel's salvific appearance "at a small village in the woods, more than thirty miles from Boston, and in its situation exceedingly lonely, and surrounded with thickets." Curiously, Scott gave the credit for saving Hadley to Richard Whalley. In the Bibliography, see Waverly 1823, which scolded Scott's imperfect grasp of our history. However, the American Tudor 1815 wrongly said Stiles credited Dixwell with Hadley's rescue. The act, not the agent, caught people's attention.

"It must be a noble sight," said Julian, "to behold the slumbering energies of a great mind awakened into energy, and to see it assume the authority which is its due over spirits more meanly endowed."

"I once witnessed," said Bridgenorth, "something to the same effect; and as the tale is brief, I will tell it you, if you will:-

"Amongst my wanderings, the Transatlantic settlements have not escaped me; more especially the country of New England, into which our native land has shaken from her lap, as a drunkard flings from him his treasures, so much that is precious in the eyes of God and of His children. There thousands of our best and most godly men—such whose righteousness might come of cities—are content to be the inhabitants of the desert, rather encountering the unenlightened savages, than stooping to extinguish, under the oppression practised in Britain, the light that is within their own minds. There I remained for a time, during the wars which the colony maintained with Philip, a great Indian Chief, or Sachem, as they were called, who seemed a messenger sent from Satan to buffet them. His cruelty was great—his dissimulation profound; and the skill and promptitude with which he maintained a destructive and desultory warfare, inflicted many dreadful calamities on the settlement. I was, by chance, at a small village in the woods, more than thirty miles from Boston, and in its situation exceedingly lonely, and surrounded with thickets. Nevertheless, there was no idea of any danger from the Indians at that time, for men trusted to the protection of a considerable body of troops who had taken the field for protection of the frontiers, and who lay, or were supposed to lie, betwixt the hamlet and the enemy's country. But they had to do with a foe, whom the devil himself had inspired at once with cunning and cruelty. It was on a Sabbath morning, when we had assembled to take sweet counsel together in the Lord's house. Our temple was but constructed of wooden logs; but when shall the chant of trained hirelings, or the sounding of tin and brass tubes amid the aisles of a minster, arise so sweetly to Heaven, as did the psalm in which we united at once our voices and our hearts! An excellent worthy, who now sleeps in the Lord, Nehemia Solsgrace, long the companion of my pilgrimage, had just begun to wrestle in prayer, when a woman, with disordered looks and dishevelled hair, entered our chapel in a distracted manner, screaming incessantly, 'The Indians! The Indians!'-- In that land no man dares separate himself from his means of defence; and whether in the city or in the field, in the ploughed land or the forest, men keep beside them their weapons, as did the Jews at the rebuilding of the Temple. So we sallied forth with our guns and pikes, and heard the whoop of these incarnate devils, already in possession of a part of the town, and exercising their cruelty on the few whom weighty causes or indisposition had withheld from public worship; and it was remarked as a judgment, that, upon that bloody Sabbath, Adrian Hanson, a Dutchman, a man well enough disposed towards man, but whose mind was altogether given to worldly gain, was shot and scalped as he was summing his weekly gains in his warehouse. In fine, there was much damage done; and although our arrival and entrance into combat did in some sort put them back, yet being surprised and confused, and having no appointed leader of our band, the devilish enemy shot hard at us and had some advantage. It was pitiful to hear the screams of women and children amid the report of guns and the whistling of bullets, mixed with the ferocious yells of these savages, which they term their war-whoop. Several houses in the upper part of the village were soon on fire; and the roaring of the flames, and crackling of the great beams as they blazed, added to the horrible confusion; while the smoke which the wind drove against us gave farther advantage to the enemy, who fought as it were, invisible, and under cover, whilst we fell fast by their unerring fire. In this state of confusion, and while we were about to adopt the desperate project of evacuating the village, and, placing the women and children in the centre, of attempting a retreat to the nearest settlement, it pleased Heaven to send us unexpected assistance. A tall man, of a reverend appearance, whom no one of us had ever seen before, suddenly was in the midst of us, as we hastily agitated the resolution of retreating. His garments were of the skin of the elk, and he wore sword and carried gun; I never saw anything more august than his features, overshadowed by locks of grey hair, which mingled with a long beard of the same colour. 'Men and brethren,' he said, in a voice like that which turns back the flight, 'why sink your hearts? and why are you thus disquieted? Fear ye that the God we serve will give you up to yonder heathen dogs? Follow me, and you shall see this day that there is a captain in Israel!' He uttered a few brief but distinct orders, in a tone of one who was accustomed to command; and such was the influence of his appearance, his mien, his language, and his presence of mind, that he was implicitly obeyed by men who had never seen him until that moment. We were hastily divided, by his orders, into two bodies; one of which maintained the defence of the village with more courage than ever, convinced that the Unknown was sent by God to our rescue. At his command they assumed the best and most sheltered positions for exchanging their deadly fire with the Indians; while, under cover of the smoke, the stranger sallied from the town, at the head of the other division of the New England men, and, fetching a circuit, attacked the Red Warriors in the rear. The surprise, as is usual amongst savages, had complete effect; for they doubted not that they were assailed in their turn, and placed betwixt two hostile parties by the return of a detachment from the provincial army. The heathens fled in confusion, abandoning the half-won village, and leaving behind them such a number of their warriors, that the tribe hath never recovered its loss. Never shall I forget the figure of our venerable leader, when our men, and not they only, but the women and children of the village, rescued from the tomahawk and scalping-knife, stood crowded around him, yet scarce venturing to approach his person, and more minded, perhaps, to worship him as a descended angel, than to thank him as a fellow-mortal. 'Not unto me be the glory,' he said; 'I am but an implement, frail as yourselves, in the hand of Him who is strong to deliver. Bring me a cup of water, that I may allay my parched throat, ere I essay the task of offering thanks where they are most due.' I was nearest to him as he spoke, and I gave into his hand the water he requested. At that moment we exchanged glances, and it seemed to me that I recognised a noble friend whom I had long since deemed in glory; but he gave me no time to speak, had speech been prudent. Sinking on his knees, and signing us to obey him, he poured forth a strong and energetic thanksgiving for the turning back of the battle, which, pronounced with a voice loud and clear as a war-trumpet, thrilled through the joints and marrow of the hearers. I have heard many an act of devotion in my life, had Heaven vouchsafed me grace to profit by them; but such a prayer as this, uttered amid the dead and the dying, with a rich tone of mingled triumph and adoration, was beyond them all — it was like the song of the inspired prophetess who dwelt beneath the palm-tree between Ramah and Bethel. He was silent; and for a brief space we remained with our faces bent to the earth—no man daring to lift his head. At length we looked up, but our deliverer was no longer amongst us; nor was he ever again seen in the land which he had rescued."

I doubted not then, as I doubt not now, that I looked on the living form of one, who had indeed powerful reasons to conceal him in the cleft of the rock."

"Are these reasons a secret?" said Julian Peveril.

"Not properly a secret," replied Bridgenorth; "for I fear not thy betraying what I might tell thee in private discourse; and besides, wert thou so base, the prey lies too distant for any hunters to whom thou couldst point out its traces. But the name of this worthy will sound harsh in thy ear, on account of one action of his life—being his accession to a great measure, which made the extreme isles of the earth to tremble. Have you never heard of Richard Whalley?"

"Of the regicide?" exclaimed Peveril, starting.

"Call his act what thou wilt," said Bridgenorth; "he was not less the rescuer of that devoted village, that, with other leading spirits of the age, he sat in the judgment-seat when Charles Stewart was arraigned at the bar, and subscribed the sentence that went forth upon him."

"I have ever heard," said Julian, in an altered voice, and colouring deeply, "that you, Master Bridgenorth, with other Presbyterians, were totally averse to that detestable crime, and were ready to have made joint-cause with the Cavaliers in preventing so horrible a parricide."

"If it were so," said Bridgenorth, "we have been richly rewarded by his successor."

"Rewarded!" exclaimed Julian; "does the distinction of good and evil, and our obligation to do the one and forbear the other, depend on the reward which may attach to our actions?"

"God forbid," answered Bridgenorth; "yet those who view the havoc which this house of Stewart have made in the Church and State—the tyranny which they exercise over men's persons and consciences—may well doubt whether it be lawful to use weapons in their defence. Yet you hear me not praise, or even vindicate the death of the King, though so far deserved, as he was false to his oath as a Prince and Magistrate. I only tell you what you desired to know, that Richard Whalley, one of the late King's judges, was he of whom I have just been speaking. I knew his lofty brow, though time had made it balder and higher; his grey eye retained all its lustre; and though the grizzled beard covered the lower part of his face, it prevented me not from recognising him. The scent was hot after him for his blood; but by the assistance of those friends whom Heaven had raised up for his preservation, he was concealed carefully, and emerged only to do the will of Providence in the matter of that battle. Perhaps his voice may be heard in the field once more, should England need one of her noblest hearts."

"Now, God forbid!" said Julian.

"Amen," returned Bridgenorth. "May God avert civil war, and pardon those whose madness would bring it on us!"

(Scott 1822, chapter 14, pages 108-11)

How Hadley Recalls the
Regicides Today

Instead of recalling other Hadley notables such as General Joseph Hooker, musician Roger Sessions or naturalist Clarence Hawkes, the town remembers the two Puritan fugitives with its street signs. If General Goffe were to reappear at this crossing, his senses would reel. Nearby he would find a Polish cafe, auto repair shops, a donut maker and a ballet school. Also, he might rightly ask, "What is a railroad? Is it necessary for salvation?"

Figure 36: Street sign near Hadley center memorializing Goffe.

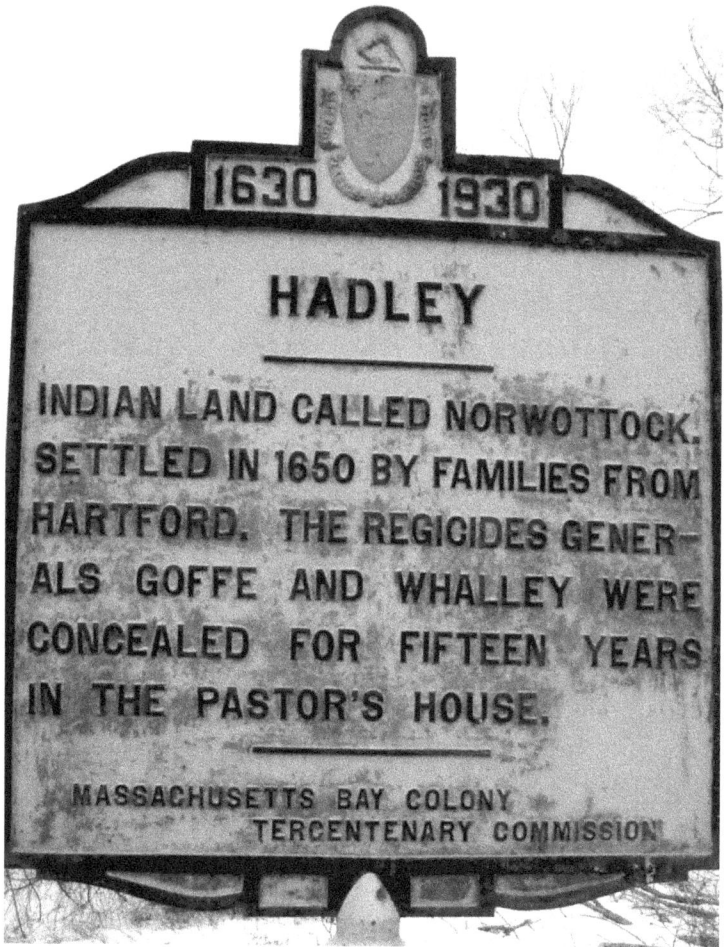

Figure 37: Scenic and peaceful Hadley introduces itself to visitors crossing the Connecticut River from Northampton on the Calvin Coolidge Memorial Bridge with this weathered marker on the north side. Yet how many people today know that these men helped behead Charles I in 1649?

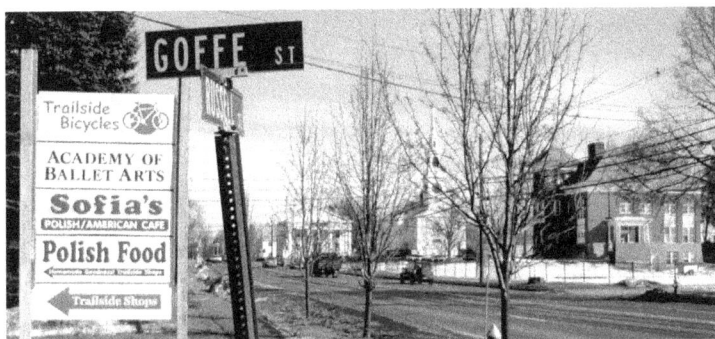

Figure 38: Sign at the south end of Goffe Street and state route 9 (Russell Street).

Goffe might feel comfortable appearing on this sign with John Russell, the pastor who concealed him in the parsonage once located about one-quarter mile to the west. Also, he would appreciate (from left to right) the town hall, the First Congregational Church and the former Russell School, further to the east on the busy road to Amherst. Those buildings confirm the Puritan trust in a necessary partnership between state, church and education.

Figure 39: A street sign at the corner of state route 9, to the west of the Goffe sign.

In the days of Goffe and his father-in-law, Edward Whalley, any Roman Catholic church, even one as handsome as St. John's, would have disturbed their religious convictions. They worshipped in an unadorned meeting house, not a consecrated structure. Church to them meant the group of believers. Only the minimally adorned Congregational Church in the town center might have soothed their anxieties. Then again, the constant doctrinal disputes of the seventeenth century might have made them equally dissatisfied with their Protestant coreligionists.

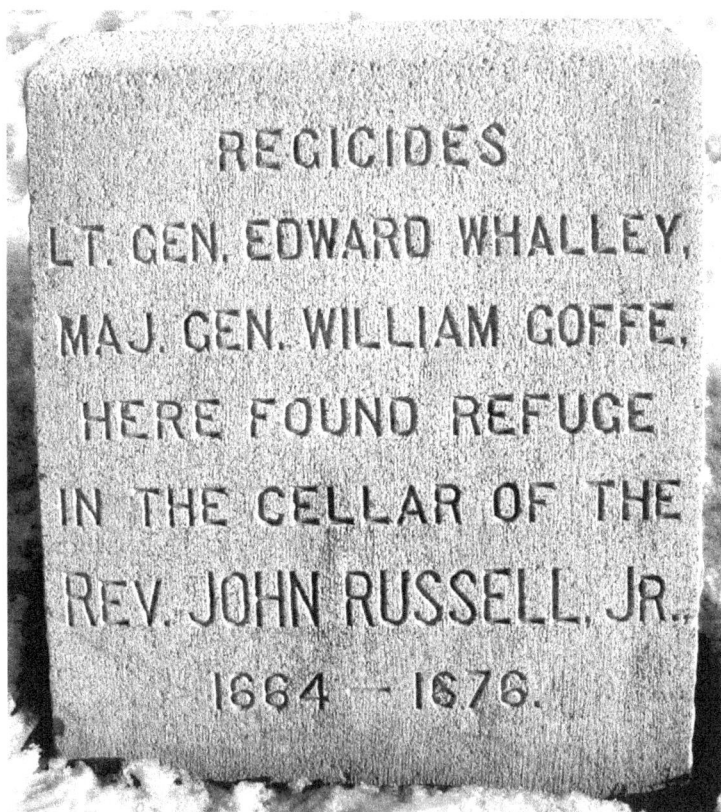

Figure 40: At the intersection of route 9 and West Street, a granite boulder marks the spot where Goffe and Whalley (and for a time John Dixwell) "found refuge in the cellar of the Rev. John Russell, Jr. 1664-1678." Here, too, the nearby manicure salon, workout center and photographic studio would disorient the three serious patriots.

The Angel and
Modern Memory

Times change and so do a society's needs. For Goffe and his generation, saving the individual soul from sin and of the group from Native Americans was paramount. The seriousness of these goals encouraged extreme mechanisms: repression of personal freedoms in communities, pitiless crusades against opponents and a continual search for both enemies and redeemers. Unlike the completely fictional champions who consoled Americans during later eras of uncertainty—Dick Tracy or Superman— William Goffe emerged as a kind of amphibian who was certainly a verifiable leader and perhaps a preserver of his town. Because battle has not raged near us since the Civil War, we may not feel how the urgent craving for peace led earlier readers to accept the two persons as one.

Is the Angel still worth recalling? A gloomy article two centuries after his era speculated, "the days of the regicides, the French and Indian wars, the Revolution, the youth of Joe Hooker – these are the reminiscences that cling about the Hadley of to- day. The Hadley of a generation hence will not be the same peaceful, wide-avenued place of 1887. The long vistas of elms will have departed…. No more, as in ancient Rome, will the noontide hour see a deserted street. The shriek of the engine will awaken the dwellers to the activity of the outside world. The world itself will invade these sacred precincts for profit and for recreation.... [S]he might well wish to turn her face to the wall and die." (Hadley's Many Memories 1887, page 11.) Obviously, some of these changes have come about, but how substantial have they been?

Readers with a philosophical interest may contradict the previous generalization and invoke the old saying, "the more things change, the more they remain the same." I recall the stirring plea by Senator Albert J. Beveridge of Indiana for America to build an empire.

> Mr. President, this question is deeper than any question of party politics; deeper than any question of the isolated policy of our country even; deeper even than any question of constitutional power. It is elemental. It is racial. God has not been preparing the English-speaking and Teutonic peoples for a thousand years for nothing but vain and idle self-contemplation and self-admiration. No! He has made us the master organizers of the world to establish system where chaos reigns. He has given us the spirit of progress to overwhelm the forces of reaction throughout the earth. He has made us adepts in government that we may administer government among savage and senile peoples. Were it not for such a force as this the world would relapse into barbarism and night. And of all our race He has marked the American people as His chosen nation to finally lead in the regeneration of the world. This is the divine mission of America, and it holds for us all the profit, all the glory, all the happiness possible to man. We are trustees of the world's progress, guardians of its righteous peace. The judgment of the Master is upon us: "Ye have been faithful over a few things; I will make you ruler over many things." (Beveridge 1900)

His words might have emerged from any number of Goffe's contemporaries. True, by the late nineteenth century, conscience-struck thinkers like Mark Twain, Rudyard Kipling, Andrew Carnegie and William Jennings Bryan opposed this declaration of war against non-"Teutonic" peoples. However, like Old Testament Hebrews and seventeenth-century Puritans, most citizens of the United States supported this appeal for a crusade. Using various pious excuses, it overthrew democratic governments in Hawaii, the Philippines, central and south America.

It is small comfort to note how our country's smug adventurism, then and now, sadly resembled that of many nations. To give only a single representative example, as I concluded this study, history repeated itself with an eerie similarity to the events in Goffe's time: *The Boston Globe* featured a three-column picture of West Bank settlers in Israel denouncing the government's plan to accommodate Palestinians. The aggrieved majority carry signs in a demonstration, one of which reads, "God's Bible gave Us this land." (Settlers 2009)

The injustices of oppression may always plague people. The legend of the Angel of Hadley shows that the victors in a cultural conflict can easily rationalize, even glorify, acts that neutral observers would rightly condemn. Having agreed that those with power try to keep and extend it, we can also admit the exploits of that distant year can stir us. On some deep psychic level, we want to be on the side of right and will accept almost any proof that our cause has more merit than that of our appointed enemy. Thus the story of the Hunted Man, the Stranger, the Angel of Hadley deserves to be retold in every generation.

Bibliography

The following works fall into two categories. Some help us understand the imaginative world of Goffe, his predecessors and his successors. Others specifically mention the Angel incident. Authors have used Goffe for different purposes. They scolded rebels (Hutchinson 1765), praised revolutionaries (Stiles 1793), condemned Puritan excesses (McHenry 1823), expanded romantic possibilities (Herbert 1845), promoted current research methods (Dexter 1876), flattered readers that they had noble ancestors (Robbins 1869) or supplied quaint information for travelers (Roberts 1906; Marlowe 1945). A substantial number mentioned the Angel for local color (Nason 1874). Taken together, these many references demonstrate the story's remarkable adaptability to diverse audiences.

Spelling and punctuation generally retain their original forms. The major orthographic changes are inserting modern capital letters in titles and transcribing VV as W (nevvs becomes news), v as u (vse becomes use) and long ſ as s (leſſ becomes less).

If you wish to see the full text of a particular work, you might be able to access it electronically. For books and pamphlets published 1475-1700, consult Early English Books Online; for works published 1701-1800, consult Eighteenth Century Books Online; for later works, consult Project Gutenberg or Google Books.

NUREMBERG 1493

Hartmann Schedel (1440-1514), author; Michael Wolgemut (c. 1435-1519) and Wilhelm Pleydenwurff (c. 1460-1494), artists, "The Universe Governed by God." *Liber Chronicarum* [Nuremberg Chronicles] (Nuremberg: Anton Kroberger, 1493).

Described and pictured on page 8.

GENEVA BIBLE 1560

The Bible and Holy Scriptures (Geneva: Rouland Hall, 1560) title page.

Described and pictured on pages 12-13.

CALVIN 1564

Jean Calvin, "Letter to the Duchess of Ferrara." *Letters.* Ed. Bonnet, Trans. M. R. Gilchrist (Philadelphia: Presbyterian Board of Publications, 1854).

Quoted on page 14.

CASE 1588

"Elizabeth I as Part of the Natural Order of the Universe." John Case, *Sphaera Civitatis* [The Spheres of Government] (London, Joseph Barnes, 1588) frontpiece.

Described and pictured on pages 9-10.

MORRELL 1625

William Morrell, *New-England. Or A Briefe Ennaration of the Ayre, Earth, Water, Fish and Fowles of that Country. With a Description of the Natures, Orders, Habits, and Religion of the Natives; In Latine and English Verse* (London: I. D., 1625) passim.

Quoted on pages 27-28.

VINCENT 1637

Philip Vincent (1600-?), *A True Relation of the Late Battell Fought in New England, Between the English, and the Salvages* (London: M. P., 1637).

Mentioned on page 41.

VINCENT 1638

Philip Vincent, *The Lamentations of Germany. Wherein, as in a Glasse, We May Behold Her Miserable Condition, and Reade the Woefull Effects of Sinne* (London: E. Griffin, 1638) 9.

Described and pictured on pages 16-17.

UNDERHILL 1638

John Underhill (died 1672) and R. H., *Newes from America; or, A New and Experimentall Discoverie of New England; Containing, a True Relation of their War-like Proceedings these Two Yeares last past, with a Figure of the Indian fort, or Palizado. Also a Discovery of these Places, that as yet have very Few or no Inhabitants Which would yeeld Speciall Accommodation to such as will Plant there, Viz. Queenapoik. Agu-wom. Hudsons River. Long Island. Nahanticut. Martins Vinyard. Pequet. Naransett Bay. Elizabeth Islands. Puscat away. Casko with about a Hundred Islands neere to Casko* (London: I. D[awson] for Peter Cole, 1638) frontpiece.

Pictured on page 42.

CROUCH 1640

Humphrey Crouch (fl. 1635-1671), "A Whip for the Back of a Backsliding Brownist" (London: Humphrey Chrouch [sic], 1640).

BRADFORD PRE-1646

William Bradford (c. 1588-1657), *History of Plymouth Plantation. 1606-1646*. Ed.William T. Davis (New York: Charles Scribner's Sons, 1908) 96.

Quoted on page 27.

CATALOGUE 1647

Illustration for the broadside "A Catalogue of the Severall Sects and Opinions in England and Other Nations. With a Briefe Rehearsall of their State and Dangerous Tenents" (? London: R. A., 1647).

Pictured on page 18.

FEATLEY 1647

Illustration by W. M. for Daniel Featley (1582-1645), *The Dippers Dipt, or, The Anabaptists Duck'd and Plung'd over Head and Ears, at a Disputation in Southwark also a Large and Full Discourse of their 1. Originall, 2. Severall Sorts, 3. Peculiar Errours, 4. High Attempts against the State, 5. Capitall Punishments* (London: N.B. and Richard Royston, 1647) 25.

Described and pictured on pages 17-18.

ENGLANDS WOLFE 1647

"Englands Wolfe with Eagle Clawes or The Cruell Impieties of Bloud-thirsty Royalists, and Blasphemous Anti-Parliamentarians, under the Command of that Inhumane Prince Rupert, Digby, and the Rest. Wherein the Barbarous Crueltie of Our Civill Unciville Warres is Briefly Discovered" (London: Matthew Simmons, 1647).

Pictured on page 20.

MARSHALL 1649

William Marshall (1617-49) engraving. ΈΙΚΩΝ ΒΑΣΙΛΙΚΗ [Eikon Basilike]. *The True Pourtracture of His Sacred Majestie in His Solitudes and Sufferings. With a Perfect Copy of Prayers Used by His Majesty in the Time of His Sufferings* (London: np, 1649) frontpiece.

Described and pictured on pages 24-25.

JOHNSON 1654

Edward Johnson (1599-1672), *A History of New-England. From the English Planting in theYeere 1628, until the Yeere 1652. The*

Wonder-Working Providence of Sion's Savior in New England (London: Nath[aniel] Brooke, 1654) 173.

Quoted on page 32.

FAIRTHORNE 1658

William Fairthorne (1616-1691), "The Emblem of Englands Distractions as also Her Attained and Expected Freedom and Happiness" (London, 1658).

Described and pictured on pages 23-24.

REBELS NO SAINTS 1661

A Person of Quality, *Rebels No Saints: or, a Collection of the Speeches, Private Passages, Letters and Prayers of those Persons Lately Executed . . . Wherein Their Pretended Sanctity is Refuted, and a Further Inspection Made into the Lives and Practices of those Unhappy and Traiterous Politicians* (London: nd;, 1661) frontpiece.

Gloating over the horrific judicial murders of former Puritan officials condemned after the Restoration of Charles I.

Pictured on page 25.

CAUSE OF GOD 1663

John Higginson (1616-1710), *The Cause of God and His People in New-England* (Cambridge, MA: Samuel Green, 1663) 10.

This optimistic vision of a spiritually evolving community may have dimmed for the minister of Salem's First Church (1660-1708). He participated in the 1692 witch trials and watched as his own daughter was charged. Still, he felt that copying the Hebrews' strict codes of conduct was essential for right relations with God.

Quoted on page 11.

PEPYS PRE-1669

Samuel Pepys (1633-1703), *Memoirs ... Comprising His Diary*. Ed. Richard Lord Braybrooke (London: Frederick Warner, post 1825) 55.

No mention of Goffe. Comment on Judge Harrison's execution.

Quoted on page 36.

MATHER 1674; 1676

Increase Mather (1639-1723), *A Brief History of the Warr with the Indians in New-England. (From June 24. 1675. When the First English-man was Murdered by the Indians, to August 12. 1676. When Philip, aliis Metacomet, the Principal Author and Beginner of the Warr, was Slain.) Wherein the Grounds, Beginning, and Progress of the Warr, is Summarily Expressed. Together with a Serious Exhortation to the Inhabitants of that Land* (Boston: John Foster, 1676) 7-8. Reprinted London: Richard Chiswell, 1676) 7-8.

First crucial hint about Hadley incident.

Quoted on pages 47-48 from the London edition.

SELLER 1675

John Seller (c. 1630-1697), Detail from "A Mappe of New England ... to bee Sold at his Shop at the Hermitage in Wapping And by John Hills in Exchange Alley in Cornhill London." Included in *Atlas Maritimus, or Sea Atlas* (1675).

Described and pictured on page 35.

BRIEF AND TRUE NARRATION 1675

A Brief and True Narration of the Late Wars Risen in New-England: Occasioned by the Quarrelsom Disposition, and Perfidious Carriage of the Barbarous, Savage and Heathenish Natives there (London: J.S., 1675).

The author wrote about the events of 7 September 1675 and mentioned Hadley, but did not refer to the rescue.

Quoted on page vi.

THOMSON 1676

Benjamin Tompson (1642-1714), *New Englands Crisis, or, A Brief Narrative of New-Englands Lamentable Estate at Present, Compar'd with the Former [but Few] Years of Prosperity Occasioned by Many Unheard of Cruelties Practised upon the*

Persons and Estates of its United Colonyes ... : Poetically Described by a Well Wisher to his Countrey (Boston: John Foster, 1676) 1; 6.

No record of the Hadley incident.

Mentioned on page 53.

SALTONSTALL 1676

Nathaniel Saltonstall (1639-1707), *The Present State of New-England; Being a Continued Account of the Bloudy Indian-War, from March till August, 1676... Together with a Catalogue of the Losses in the Whole, Sustained on Either Side, Since the Said War Began, as Near as can be Collected* (London: Dorman Newman, 1676) title page.

No record of the Hadley incident.

Mentioned on page 52.

SALTONSTALL 1676 A

Nathaniel Saltonstall, *A New and Further Narrative of the State of New-England; Being a Continued Account of the Bloudy Indian-War, from March till August, 1676, Giving a Perfect Relation of the Several Devastations, Engagements, and Transactions There: as also the Great Successes Lately Obtained Against the Barbarous Indians ... Together with a Catalogue of the Losses in the Whole, Sustaining on Either Side Since the Said War Began, as Near as can be Collected* (London: Dorman Newman, 1676) 14.

No record of the Hadley incident.

Mentioned on page 51.

SALTONSTALL 1676 B

Nathaniel Saltonstall, *A Continuation of the State of New-England. Being a Farther Account of the Indian Warr, And of the Engagement Betwixt the Joynt Forces of the United English Collonies and the Indians on the 19th of December 1675* (London: Dorman Newman, 1676) 14

No record of the Hadley incident.

Mentioned on page 52.

HUBBARD 1677

William Hubbard (1621/2-1704), *A Narrative of the Troubles with the Indians in New-England, from the First Planting Thereof in the Year 1607, to this Present Year 1677, but Chiefly of the Late Troubles in the Two Last Years, 1675 and 1676* (Boston: John Foster, 1677).

No record of the Hadley incident.

Mentioned on page 49.

HUBBARD 1677A

"A Map of New-England." William Hubbard (1621/2-1704), *The Present State of New-England. Being a Narrative of the Troubles with the Indians in New-England, from the First Planting thereof in the Year 1607, to this Present 1677: But Chiefly of the Late Troubles in the Two Last Years 1675, and 1676. To which is added a Discourse about the War with the Pequods in the Year1637* (London: Tho[mas] Parkhurst, 1677) before 1.

Pictured on page 35.

HUTCHINSON 1677

Richard Hutchinson (1602-1682), *the Warr in New-England visibly ended. King Philip that Barbarous Indian Now Beheaded, and Most of his Bloudy Adherents Submitted to Mercy, the Rest Fled far up into the Countrey, which hath given the inhabitants Encouragement to Prepare for their Settlement* (London: J.B., 1677).

Brief note for the Salem resident claiming the defeat of the Natives signified that "the Providence of God wonderfully appeared." No mention of the Hadley rescue.

Quoted on page 22.

PLAN 1678

"Plan for Seizing and Carrying to New-York Coll. Wm. Goffe the Regicide, As Set Forth in the Affidavit of John London, Apr. 20, 1678." Ed. Franklin Benjamin Hough (1822-1885). (Albany: Weed, Parsons, 1855).

An order from "Sr. Edmond Andross Governor of N: Yorke" to "apprehend & in safe custody to convay them" back to New York. The "them" are "Captn Jos. Bull & his sons" of Hartford who reputedly were sheltering Goffe under the alias of "Mr. Cooke." Mentioned on page 26.

AT A COUNCIL HELD AT BOSTON 1678

"At a Council Held at Boston the 22d. of August 1678" (Cambridge, MA: Samuel Green, 1678).

No record of the Hadley incident.

Quoted on page 50.

CHURCH 1716

Thomas Church (1639-1718), *The Entertaining History of King Philip's War, which Began in the Month of June, 1675.... with some Account of the Divine Providence Towards. Col. Benjamin Church.* 2nd edition (Boston: Solomon Southwick, 1716). I quote from the edition annotated by Samuel G. Drake: *The History of Philip's War, Commonly Called the Great Indian War, of 1675 and 1676.* 2nd edition (Exeter: NH: J & B Williams, 1843) iii; 244.

Benjamin Church (1639-1718) seemed to be everywhere during the conflict. He does not mention the Angel, but his editor Drake summarized Stiles' account (54), adding that Goffe may have appeared on 19 October 1675 (55). Drake also criticized the gaps in Hutchinson (iii).

Quoted on page 38.

POWNALL 1761

Thomas Pownall (1722-1805), "A Design to Represent the Beginning and Completion of an American Farm." *Six Remarkable Views in the Province of New York, New Jersey, and Pennsylvania, in North America. Sketched on the Spot by His Excellency Governor Pownall, Painted by Mr. Paul Sandby, and Engraved by Mess. Sandby, Elliot, Benazet, etc.* (London: T. Jeffreys, 1761).

Pictured on page 31.

HUTCHINSON 1765; 1828

Thomas Hutchinson (1711-1780), *History of the Colony and Province of Massachusetts-Bay* (London: M. Richardson, 1765) 1.218. Hutchinson's third volume with the footnote was published posthumously (Ed. John Hutchinson. London: John Murray, 1828, page 215).

Not everyone approved of Hutchinson's thoroughness. Samuel Drake, who edited Benjamin Church's memoirs of Philip's War, sniffed, "The lamentable manner in which Hutchinson in his History of Massachusetts passed over the Indian wars, causes us much regret, and a desire to catch at every thing that can give any light upon them" (CHURCH 1716, page iii).

Quoted on page 61.

HISTORY OF CONNECTICUT 1781

"History of Connecticut; From a Work Just Published by a Gentleman of that Province." *Political Magazine & Parliamentary, Naval, Military & Literary Journal* 2 (1 October 1781) 592.

No mention of Goffe.

Quoted on page 32.

BELKNAP 1784

Jeremy Belknap (1744-1798), *The History of New-Hampshire. Comprehending the Events of One Complete Century from the Discovery of the River Pascataqua.* Vol. 1 (1784. Dover, NH: O. Crosby and J. Varney, 1812).

Belknap bravely tried to rehabilitate the Indians by pointing to their virtues (they did not rape) and to the vices of newcomers (white sailors drowned a Native baby). Like a scholastic debater, he offered negative stereotypes usually flung at the original inhabitants (cruel, torturers, revengeful, treacherous, jealous, hatred) and then supplied examples of these incivilities from the English.

Quoted on page vi.

STILES 1793

Philagathos [Ezra Stiles], *A Poem Commemorative of Goffe, Whaley, & Dixwell, Three of the Judges of Charles I. Who, at the Restoration, took Refuge and Died in America* (Boston: Samuel Hall, 1793) 22.

Quoted on page 67.

STILES 1794

Ezra Stiles (1727-95), *History of Three of the Judges of King Charles I. Major-General Whalley, Major-General Goffe, and Colonel Dixwell: Who, at the Restoration, 1660, Fled to America; and were Secreted and Concealed, in Massachusetts and Connecticut, for near Thirty Years* (Hartford, CT: Elisha Babcock, 1794) 29; Hutchinson's footnote, 109-10.

Quoted on page 65; maps pictured on 68.

LINCOLN 1795

Benjamin Lincoln (1733-1810), "Observations on the Indians of North-America; Containing an Answer to Some Remarks of Doctor Ramsay, Published in the Collections of the Historical Society from 1795, page 99" (Boston: Massachusetts Historical Society, vol. 5, first series, 1795) 6-12.

Quoted on pages 45-46.

TRUMBULL 1797

Benjamin Trumbull (1735-1820), *A Complete History of Connecticut, Civil and Ecclesiastical, from the Emigrations of its First Planters from England, in MDCXXX, to MDCCXIII* (Hartford: Hudson & Goodwin, 1797) 1.349.

No mention of Goffe.

Mentioned on pages 37-38.

NOBLE 1798

Mark Noble (1754-1827), *The Lives of the English Regicides, and Other Commissioners of the Pretended High Court of Justice,*

Appointed to Sit in Judgment upon their Sovereign, King Charles the First (London: John Stockdale, 1798) 256.

Mention of Goffe but not of rescue.

Quoted on page 62.

HOLMES 1798

Abiel Holmes (1763-1837), *The Life of Ezra Stiles, D. D. LL.D. A Fellow of the American Philosophical Society; of the American Academy of Arts; of the Connecticut Academy of Arts and Sciences; A Corresponding Member of the Massachusetts Historical Society; Professor of Ecclesiastical History; and President of Yale College* (Boston: Thomas & Andrews, May, 1798).

A reverential biography by one of Stiles' students and son-in-law. Father of Oliver Wendell Holmes. No specific mention of the rescue. Reprinted the usual justification for having been silent about the New England careers of the three regicides until the eighteenth century's last decade: "The reason for secrecy no longer operating, since the Independence of America, had become established, and the graves of the enemies of the tyrants were sure of protection, if not of veneration; the difficulty of obtaining the history of these Judges became sensibly diminished. The task, which, twenty years before, would have been impracticable, was now undertaken."

JANSON 1807

Charles William Janson, *The Stranger in America: Containing Observations Made During a Long Residence in That Country, on the Genius, Manners and customs of the People of the United States; With Biographical Particulars of Public Characters; Hints and Facets Relative to the Arts, Sciences, Commerce, Agriculture, Manufactures, Emigrations and The Slave Trade* (London: Cundee, 1807).

It is easier to read reviews of this ponderous work than Janson's original. "Art. VII. *The Stranger in America.*" *The Edinburgh Review Or Critical Journal* 10:19 (April, 1807) 103-116 called it a "most ill arranged volume ... a most hasty performance; by a person neither accustomed to laborious composition, nor qualified to write." The reviewer quoted Janson's Angel passage at length, remarking that it was perhaps the most interesting of the other "anecdotes, facts, declamations, pictures, quotation … thrown together by a sort of manual exertion."

A second review, "*The Stranger in America.*" *Belle Assemblee; or Court and Fashionable Magazine* 2.18 (July 1807) 12-14, also provided a substantial excerpt about Goffe and Whalley to show the book is "ill arranged, and too bulky [550 pages]." Janson's brief notice of the rescue narrative implied that it was already known. Janson added that the disappearance was motivated by the regicides' "caution to prevent a discovery of their retreat."

A third review of Janson likewise criticized his loquacity and his methods: "he carelessly reflected inaccurate rumor and gossip." Philip Davidson, review of the reprinted *Stranger in America,* edited by Carl S. Driver (New York: Press of the Pioneers, 1935). *The Journal of Southern History* 2.4 (November 1936) 531.

Mentioned on page 67.

AMERICAN ANNALS 1805

Abiel Holmes, *American Annals; or, a Chronological History of America from its Discovery in MDCCCXCII to MDCCCVI* (Cambridge, MA: W. Hilliard, 1805) 1.423-24.

See Holmes 1798 for more details about Ezra Stiles' biographer and the following entry for a contemporary review. In his retelling of the rescue, Holmes paraphrased Stiles. Holmes dated the attack 1 September 1675, saying it coincided with another assault on Deerfield.

> Hadley was alarmed by the Indians in the time of public worship, and the people thrown into the utmost confusion; but the enemy was repulsed by the valour and good conduct of an aged, venerable man, who, suddenly appearing in the midst of the affrighted inhabitants, put himself at their head; led them to the onset; and, after the dispersion of the enemy, instantly disappeared. This deliverer of Hadley, then imagined to be an angel, was general Goffe, one of the judges of Charles I, who was, at the time, concealed in the town.

REVIEW OF AMERICAN ANNALS 1809

Anonymous review of Abiel Holmes, *American Annals; or, a Chronological History of America from its Discovery in 1492 to 1806* (Cambridge, MA: W. Hilliard, 1805). *Quarterly Review* 2.4 (November 1809) 319-37.

By this date, the Angel story was widely known. Although the reviewer (unfairly, in my opinion) called Holmes' book "meager and miserably imperfect," it did retell the Regicides' tale clearly. Although Whalley probably was developing senile dementia in the 1670s, Goffe retained enough vigor to lead the Hadley men against their attackers and then "was no longer found." The reviewer and Holmes satisfied the nineteenth-century's feeling that their morals had improved from Puritan days by reminding the audience, "The prevalent opinion … among all sects of Christians at that day, that toleration is sinful, ought to be remembered." Goffe would have understood the ethical imperative to convert or kill opponents.

TUDOR 1815

William Tudor, "An Address Delivered to the Phi Beta Kappa Society, at their Anniversary Meeting at Cambridge," *North American Review* 2.4 (November 1815) 13-32.

An impassioned and patriotic appeal for American poets to use material from our country rather than from Europe. Tudor praised our landscapes and Indians as fit topics for epic. As examples he recommended the exploits of John Smith, Miles Standish and the Angel:

> The incident mentioned by President Stiles, is very striking, of Dixwell one of the regicides, suddenly emerging from his concealment, and by his presence animating an infant settlement, when suddenly assailed from the Indians, to repel the savages, and then returning unnoticed to his retreat; which made many of the people who knew nothing of his concealment regard him as a mysterious being, a good angel sent for their deliverance.

Like Scott, Tudor gives credit not to Goffe but to a second judge, John Dixwell. The action was apparently more famous than the doer. The search for suitable local subjects soon occupied the attention of Hudson River painters and influential authors. Washington Irving so felt the lack of indigenous tales that he took other nations' narratives (like the German "Peter Klaus" or early Christian "Seven Sleepers of Ephesus") to produce "Rip Van Winkle." Although Irving probably knew the Angel story, he does not use it.

Mentioned on page 79.

DWIGHT 1821

Timothy Dwight (1752-1817), *Travels; in New-England and New-York* (New-Haven: S. Converse, 1821) 1.353-54. (First published 1805.)

Quoted on pages 69-70.

SCOTT 1822

Sir Walter Scott (1771-1832), *Peveril of the Peak* (Edinburgh: Archibald Constable, 1822; London: Hurst, Robinson, 1822) chapter 14, pages 108-11.

Quoted on pages 80-84.

WAVERLY 1823

"Waverly; New-England; Hadley, Massachusetts; Indians." *The Times and Hartford Advertiser* 7.324 (11 March 1823) 3.

A paragraph noting that Scott had appropriated the Goffe story for his recent novel, but done so "imperfectly, and in many aspects incorrectly, probably from an inaccurate knowledge of our history." The patriotic reviewer insists that "the exploits of our ancestors ... and their characters [are] worthy of exalted praise."

Mentioned on page 79.

MCHENRY 1823

James McHenry (1785-1845), *The Spectre of the Forest, Or the Annals of the Housatonic. A New England Romance* (New York: Bliss and White, 1823) 2.97-99.

McHenry, a medical doctor from Ireland who studied for the Presbyterian ministry, admired Scott and became an author. Edgar Allen Poe praised one of his poems ("the only tolerable American epic") in "A Chapter on Autography [Part III]." *Graham's Magazine* 20 (January 1842) 48. McHenry edited the *American Monthly Magazine* and eventually served as US Consul at Londonderry. A scholarly overview of his life and works: Robert E. Blanc, *James McHenry (1785-1845): Playwright and Novelist* (Philadelphia: UPenn Press, 1939).

McHenry's novel showed that even a worthy person on the American frontier had to be rescued from heathens and corrupt church practices. The Goffe figure saves his daughter, who has come from England and been accused of witchcraft, by bursting into the zealots' quarters and exploiting their Puritan fear of specters. His detestation of ignorant witch hunters leads him to repair relations with William and Mary, the new moderate monarchs. As death approaches, he retires to a cave.

BARKER 1824

James Nelson Barker (1784-1858), *Superstition; or, The Fanatic Father.* The tragedy was acted at the Chestnut Street Theatre, Philadelphia, on 12 March 1824 and first printed in an edition of Lopez and Wemyss, 1826. Reprinted in *Best Plays of the Early American Theatre: From the Beginning to 1916.* Ed. John Gassner (New York: Crown, 1967). Also reprinted by Feedback Theatre Books, Brooklin, ME, 1998.

The playwright Barker adapted Scott's novel *Peveril of the Peak* as well as Hutchinson and McHenry for his drama. Barker added a second father-daughter plot but kept the witchcraft theme. After "the Unknown" calms villagers during an Algonkian assault, a fanatical church elder named Ravensworth accuses his own daughter Isabella and grandson Charles of being in league with devils. Unfortunately, the boy is executed, although Isabella reveals that Charles II had raped then secretly married her. Puritanism's mindless bigotry ruins the real chance to unite people, in this case, a scion of Puritans and Catholics. Once again, this Goffe figure hides in caves.

A useful article shows that the play contradicts Hutchinson's conservative image of Goffe as a rebel against just authority. "Barker recycled the legend to reify a Revolutionary ethos of classical *virtu* – the patriotic courage and martial valor requisite for the republic's survival…. The fanatic 'zeal' [of hypocritical Puritans] that endangers the community from within is, paradoxically, necessary to safeguard it from military invasion [by Amerindians] from without." Philip Gould, "New England Witch-Hunting and the Politics of Reason in the Early Republic." *The New England Quarterly* 68.1 (March 1995) 58-82.

ANONYMOUS WITCH 1824

Anonymous, *The Witch of New England* (Philadelphia: Lea and Carey, 1824).

SARGENT 1993 discusses this regicide-and-witchcraft play. I have not seen it.

HOYT 1824

Epaphras Hoyt (1765-1850), *Antiquarian Researches: Comprising A History of the Indian Wars in the Country Bordering Connecticut River and Parts Adjacent, and Other Interesting Events, From the First Landing of the Pilgrims, to the Conquest of Canada by the English, in 1760: With Notices of Indian Depredations in the Neighboring Country: and the First Planting and Progress of Settlements in New England, New York and Canada* (Greenfield, MA: Ansel Phelps, 1824) 82-83; 135-36.

Hoyt told how, warned that Charles' agents had arrived in Boston, Goffe and Whalley left New Haven on 13 October 1664 and, after the "tedious march of about one hundred miles" reached Reverend Russell's.

> The house of the friendly clergyman, situated on the east side of the main street, near the centre of the village, was of two stories, with a kitchen attached, and ingeniously fitted up for the reception of the judges. The east chamber was assigned for their residence, from which a door opened into a closet, back of the chimney, and a secret trap door communicated with an under closet, from which was

a private passage to the cellar, into which it was easy to descend in case of a search…. In the war with Philip, in 1675 and 1676, while the judges were in the place – soldiers billeted on the inhabitants, and vigilant officers quartered in the village, the non-discovery of the exiles is truly astonishing.

In addition, when Hoyt recounted the now familiar anecdote, he added a critical note about the date.

A curious circumstance occurred in this attack [by 700 Indians against Hadley, guarded by troops under captain Swain on 12 June 1676]. When the people were in great consternation, and rallying to oppose the Indians, a man of venerable aspect, differing from the inhabitants in his apparel, appeared, and assuming command, arrayed them in the best manner for defence, evincing much knowledge of military tactics; and by his advice and example, continued to animate the men throughout the attack. When the Indians drew off the stranger disappeared and nothing further was heard of him.

Mentioned on page 61.

O. X. 1826

O. X., "Goffe and Whaley, The Regicides." *The Worcester Magazine and Historical Journal* 1.7 (January 1826) 212-13.

In 1664, the king's commissioners arrived in Boston, with particular instructions to seek for the regicides; in consequence of which it became necessary for them to find a new asylum. [They were hiding with a Mr. Tomlin of Milford, CT.] The Rev. Mr. Russell, of Hadley, on [sic] Connecticut river then the western-most settlement in Massachusetts colony, consented to receive them… Here, and at the house of P. Tilton, Esq. Unknown to every one in the village except the respective families of these gentlemen, they lay buried in the most profound concealment for more than sixteen years.

The following is the only memorial action in which either of them was engaged during the remainder of their unhappy lives. In September, 1675, while the people of Hadley were assembled at church, they were unexpectedly surrounded and attacked by a body of Philip's Indians. The affrighted inhabitants, after having feebly repelled the attack, were on the point of yielding, when, suddenly, there appeared among them a venerable old man of singular appearance. Placing himself at their head, and animating them by his address and evidently superior knowledge in military tactics, he enabled them to make a successful resistance, and soon compelled the savages to withdraw. Immediately after the victory the stranger disappeared, and the good people of Hadley imputed this sudden and effectual interposition in their behalf, to an angel, until the fact of the judges being at that time secreted among them became known, when they ascertained that this angel, was no other than Goffe, who, seeing the inhabitants on the eve of flight, saved the village from destruction, and himself and Whaley from inevitable discovery.

COOPER 1829

James Fenimore Cooper (1759-1851), *The Wept of Wish-ton-Wish: A Tale*, 2 volumes (Philadelphia: Carey, Lea & Carey, 1829).

Cooper may have seen a performance of Barker's play – or read Scott. Anyway, his novel presented "the Stranger," later called "Submission," a regicide living at Wish-ton-Wish, a fertile valley some twenty hours' ride north of Hartford. Divided into two halves, the novel takes place in the 1660s and 1676. In both parts, Submission warns settlers that the Narragansetts are about to attack and helps the beleaguered utopians. Submission himself is alternately commanding and helpless. Four arrogant, materialistic agents of Charles II have pursued him with the same viciousness as do the Indians. At the conclusion of the novel's first section, the Indians drive Submission and the inhabitants to a blockhouse that burns to the ground. The "savages" gloat over "the smouldering pile" (Mohawk Edition, New York: G. P. Putnam's Sons, nd, chapter 15, page 189); but in the next chapter, the settlers emerge from a secure, stone-walled well beneath the blockhouse, thus preserving Submission, Faith, Content, Martha and Reuben – the Christian stalwarts. This rebirth ironically parallels the Native American legends of the world's first inhabitants who arrived from their original home under the earth by way of a tunnel to the upper land.

The next half of the novel pictured a declined community. The former leader Mark Heathcote, a pious but generous man who forgave the Indians, has yielded to the aptly named Reverend Meek Wolfe, a bigoted hypocrite. The latter preaches on the text from Judges, bellowing,

> "Lift your eyes upwards, my brethren –"

> "Rather turn them to the earth!" interrupted a deep, authoritative voice from the body of the church; "there is present need of all your faculties to save life, and even to guard the tabernacle of the Lord!" (Mohawk Edition, chapter 22, page 280).

Cooper described Submission in the expected manner: "His attire was of the simple guise and homely materials of the country.... His hand was armed with a shining broadsword, such as were then used by the cavaliers of England" (Mohawk Edition, chapter 22, pages 280-81). His military prowess cannot reverse the numerical superiority of the Indians, who capture him but, on the urging of Conanchet, release him. Submission lives in the forest, a wild locale that Cooper invests with all the respect a sophisticated tourist would have for "the narrow and water-worn vineyards and meadows which are washed by the Rhone, ere that river pours its tribute into the Lake of Leman" (Mohawk Edition, chapter 26, page 337). As a rueful admission that miscegenation cannot work, Conanchet entrusts Submission with his baby, whose mother is the kidnapped granddaughter of Heathcote, and then goes bravely to a death engineered by the fanatic Meek.

The Indians were said to imperil both life and virtue. The possibility of miscegenation troubled Anglos. In real life, many abducted white women chose to stay with their Indian tribes even when they were free to leave. By the time Cooper finished *The Wept*, Mary Jemison, "the white woman of the Genesee," had already told how after being kidnapped she lived easily and happily with the Seneca. She married twice and told her story to a rather unsympathetic listener who still could not conceal her essential contentment. (*The Life of Mrs. Mary Jemison* [Canandaigua, NY: J. D. Bemis, 1824])

In Cooper's novel, Ruth is kidnapped and married to an Indian, yet he is a paragon of decency. Given the prejudices of the time, he has to die. Cooper's uncharacteristic sympathy for Native Americans also informs four of the Leatherstocking novels. Natty Bumppo, the white adventurer known as Deerslayer, Pathfinder, Leatherstocking, "the Trapper" and Hawkeye, travels with his noble Mohican friend Chingachgook in *The Pioneers* (1823), *The Last of the Mohicans* (1826), *The Pathfinder* (1840) and *The Deerslayer* (1841). Although ideals of "the noble savage" as envisioned by Romantic theorists, both Chingachgook and his son Uncas die. The Angel story, however, had no room for such sympathy.

Mentioned on page 48.

Figure 41: Felix Octavius Carr Darley (1821-1888), Illustration.
The Wept of Wish-Ton-Wish (New York: W. A. Townsend, 1859) 212.

Darley caters to the popular fear of kidnapping by aliens. An enormously popular artist, he complemented Cooper by illustrating all 32 of his novels. In addition, he designed banknotes.

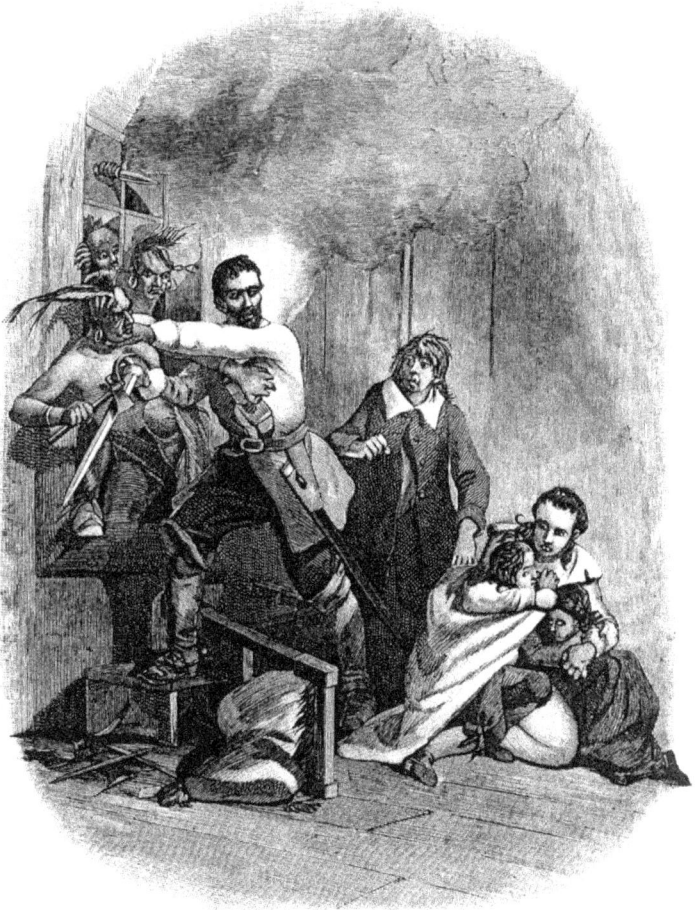

Figure 42: Anonymous wood engraving. *The Wept of Wish-Ton-Wish* (New York: Peter Fenelon Collier, 1893) 178.

The caption reads, "'To the block' shouted the steady soldier, while with a powerful arm he held the enemy in the throat of the narrow passage, stopping the approach of those in the rear by the body of his foe. 'For the love of life and children, woman, to the block.'"

White writers often framed their frontier tales as never-ending defenses by a beleaguered minority against overwhelming numbers of enemies. Cooper and the artist phrased his hero's act in terms of both Goffe's experience and that of classical protectors. Many readers who had been to school already knew of the 300 Spartans at the narrow passage of Thermopylae who held off the original barbarians (that is, people who could not speak Greek); Horatius denied the Etruscans passage over Rome's only bridge; von Winkelried gathered lances into his body so his freedom-seeking Swiss companions could break though the Hapsburg battle line. In our day, Ernest Hemingway ended *For Whom the Bell Tolls* with the American Robert Jordan guarding the retreat of his anti-Fascist Spanish comrades although his own death is certain.

BACON 1831

Delia Salter Bacon (1811-59), *Tales of the Puritans. The Regicides. The Fair Pilgrim. Castine* (New Haven: A. H. Maltby, 1831).

Best known as the proponent of Sir Francis Bacon, Sir Walter Raleigh and Edmund Spencer as the real authors of plays attributed to Shakespeare, Bacon attracted the attention of Ralph Waldo Emerson and Nathaniel Hawthorne. Although she died after a mental breakdown, this collection of stories, written in her late teens, shows controlled research. She furthers the melodramatic image of a Satan-haunted Puritan world where "a superstition more vast, and more awful hung over the glens and forests," namely dread of the fallen rebel angel by all including a pure maiden who feels him "throwing his mysterious and sinful influence even around the inmost recesses of her own heart." (45) In "Castine," a noble Indian captor named Alaska proposes marriage to Lucy Everett, who reluctantly refuses. Bacon balanced these imaginative passages by an Appendix that traced the Regicides' movements in New England. She quoted the royal agents Thomas Kellond and Thomas Kirk, Hutchinson, Stiles and Noble. She also reproduced Stiles' version of the Angel rescue, calling it "a singular and romantic incident." (292-94)

STRONG 1832

Titus Strong (1787-1855), *The Deerfield Captive, An Indian Story; Being a Narrative of Facts, for the Instruction of the Young* (Greenfield, MA: Ansel Phelps, 1832) 20.

No mention of Goffe.

Pictured on page 58.

LEAVITT 1833

Joshua Leavitt (1794-1873), *The Redeemed Captive: A Narrative of the Captivity, Sufferings, and Return of the Rev. John Williams, Minister of Deerfield, Massachusetts, Who was Taken Prisoner by the Indians On the Destruction of the Town, A. D. 1704. For Sabbath Schools* (New York: S. W. Benedict, 1833) 6.

No mention of Goffe. Quoted on pages 38-39. Leavitt's frontpiece, a woodcut by Alexander Anderson (1775-1870), showed the attack on Ensign John Sheldon's house, the "Indian House," on 29 February 1703/4 at Deerfield.

Reproduced on page 58.

GOODRICH 1833

Charles Augustus Goodrich (1790-1862), *A History of the United States of America; on a Plan Adapted to the Capacity of Youths* (Boston: Carter, Hendee, 1833) 39-40.

No mention of Goffe, but does recall the attacks in September 1675 on Hadley, Deerfield and Northampton.

HADLEY REMINISCENCES 1834

"Hadley Reminiscences." *The Brattleboro Messenger* 13.17 (16 May 1834) 1.

The anonymous author cited as his authority "Rev. Phinehas Cooke, now of Lebanon, N. H., a native of Hadley." According to Sylvester Judd, *The History of Hadley, Massachusetts* (1905. Rpt. Somersworth, NH: New Hampshire Publishing, 1976, 25), Cooke lived from 1781 to 1853. The writer of "Reminiscences" imagined the townspeople's "alarm and trepidation" as the attackers approach: "What shall we do, who will lead us? In the midst of the confusion, the stranger said, 'I will lead, -- follow me.'" They obey his directions for loading and firing an old cannon (it destroys a stone chimney and frightens away the Indians). The savior's "venerable appearance – his silver locks, and his pale visage" prompted the rumor of an angel. "Mr. Russell, who saw that no evil could arise from their credulity... favor[ed] the fancy of the people."

STONE 1834; 1844

Williasm Leet[e] Stone (1792-1844), *Tales and Sketches, Such as They Are* (New York: Harper & Brothers, 1834) 1.1-XXX. Rpt. *Mercy Disborough: A Tale of New England Witchcraft* (Bath, NY: R. L. Underhill, 1844).

Another condemnation of the 1692 witchcraft mania that curiously mixed admiration for the regicides with some sympathy for Native Americans, even though they attack. Based on an actual case in Quinnipiack, near New Haven, the novel made Mercy an appealing victim of Puritan fanaticism. Her accusers blame her for odd noises and flickering lights in Governor Leet's store house. An Amerindian assault led by the noble Onico, son of Uncas, the Mohegan king, interrupts her public burning. After the raiders withdraw, no one can find Mercy, her father or her fiancée. Twenty years later, Mercy, husband David Salsbury and their happy children are discovered living happily in the Ousatonic river valley. The mystery of the store house is solved in the mid-eighteenth century when the structure is demolished, revealing a memorial stone inscribed by Whalley and Goffe to thank Governor Leet for hiding them there from "the Vengeance of the Tyrant's Son." Their motto: "Opposition to Tyrants, is Obedience to God."

ANGEL OF HADLEY 1836

E.T., "The Angel of Hadley." *American Ladies' Magazine* 9.10 (October 1836) 555-57.

The author introduced a sentimental idea like that of Lincoln about the inevitable disappearance of Indians: "A few more moons, and like the scattered leaves/Of the departing year—whose faded pride/Their fallen race resembles—they are gone." Quoted on page 46.

THE FUGITIVE 1837

H., "The Fugitive." *Harvardiana* 3.5 (February 1837) 170-74.

An account of two lovers taking a winter walk and having their dog frightened by a stranger with a "manly brow," "past the summer of life." He identifies himself: "I am *William Goffe*—the regicide!" They give him shelter in "a secret apartment." The odd combination of romance, exile and compassion enlists the reader's sympathy for Goffe.

A prequel to Goffe's Hadley years.

PLUMMER 1838

Narrative of the Captivity and Extreme Sufferings of Mrs. Clarissa Plummer (New York: Perry and Cooke, 1838) frontpiece.

No record of the Hadley incident.

Pictured on page 40.

BARBER 1839

John Barber (1798-1885), "Hadley." *Historical Collections, Being a General Collection of Interesting Facts, Traditions, Biographical Sketches, Anecdotes, &c., Relating to the History and Antiquities of Every Town in Massachusetts, with Geographical Descriptions* (Worcester: Dorr, Howland, 1839) 323-26.

Almost the entire entry concerned Goffe and his residence in town. Barber reprinted verbatim as fact the account of an attack on 12 June 1676 from HOYT 1824.

A second reference on pages 618-19 recounted the Sergeant murders.

Cited on page 43.

A RELIC OF ANTIQUITY 1841

"A Relic of Antiquity." *The Christian Watchman* 22.3 (15 January 1841) 10-11.

Reprint of Goffe's letter sent after 29 May 1662 to his wife in England. "The story of the sudden appearance of Goffe, when the town was suddenly attacked by Indians, and the surprise of the people is well known."

HAWTHORNE 1842

Nathaniel Hawthorne (1804-1864), "The Grey Champion." *New-England Magazine* 8 (January1835) 20-26. Revised and expanded to the version we read today in *Twice-told Tales* (Boston: American Stationers' Company, 1837) 11-22.

Synopsis: One late afternoon in April 1689, Sir Edmund Andros, the vicious governor of Massachusetts under King James II, "the bigoted successor of Charles the Voluptuous," prepares to make a show of military strength before the oppressed people of Boston. He and his cavalier cronies, "being warm with wine," contrast to the crowd of stalwart citizens, fearful of another slaughter by Catholics, yet brave as the "original Puritans, when threatened by some peril of the wilderness." "Suddenly, there was seen the figure of an ancient man, who seemed to have emerged from among the people." This grey champion, with "a hoary beard that descended on his breast," "marched onward with a warrior's step." "[T]he saint, so grey, so dimly seen, in such ancient garb, could only belong to some old champion of the righteous cause, whom the oppressor's drum had summoned from his grave." With authority ("I have stayed the march of a king"), he sternly orders the royalist group to stand back and then announces that Popish James is no longer king and that Andros's power is ended. Andros quails and orders his red coats back. The old former governor, Simon Bradstreet, councils patience and later hugs the champion. Next day news comes that Protestants William and Mary have taken the throne. Andros is indeed stripped of all authority. Where is the Gray Champion? Who is he? Stories vary. He will come when freedom needs him: "His hour is one of darkness, and adversity and peril. But should domestic tyranny oppress us, or the invader's step pollute our soil, still may the Grey Champion come, for he is the type of New England's hereditary spirit, and his shadowy march on the eve of danger, must ever be the pledge that New England's sons will vindicate their ancestry."

John C. Stubbs suggests that Hawthorne was aware of other romances such as McHenry's *Spectre* (1823, mentioned above) and the later works by Herbert (mentioned below). See "Hawthorne's *The Scarlet Letter*: The Theory of the Romance and the Use of the New England Situation." *PMLA* 83.5 (October 1969) 1439-47. See also DOUBLEDAY 1962, below.

SOUTHEY 1845

Robert Southey (1774-1843), *Oliver Newman: A New-England Tale*. Ed. Herbert Hill (London: Longman, Brown, Green & Longmans, 1845).

This rambling and unfinished posthumous poem capitalized on Goffe's fame. Southey invented the title character, a Quaker son of Goffe and Whalley's daughter. The editor tried to clarify the plot by including the author's sometimes contradictory notes. The Hadley rescue was taken from Dwight. Southey used clichés about the Indians' love of revenge, animal traits, poor work ethic, cannibalism, devil worship, tolerance of pain and uselessness unless converted.

HERBERT 1845

Henry William Herbert (1807-58), *The Fair Puritan. A Romance of the Bay Province* (Boston: Henry L. Williams, 1845).

HERBERT 1845A

The Innocent Witch. A Continuation of Ruth Whalley. Or, A Romance of the Bay Province (Boston: Henry L. Williams, 1845).

I have not yet located a copy of this work.

HERBERT 1845B

The Revolt of Boston. A Continuation of Ruth Whalley. Or, A Romance of the Bay Province (Boston: Henry L. Williams, 1845). I have not yet located a copy of this work.

Best known for wearing dandified clothing and writing books about sports, Herbert created historical prose that Poe called "woefully turgid," full of "pompous grandiloquence" (Edgar Allan Poe, "A Chapter on Autography [Part I]." *Graham's Magazine* 19 [November 1841] 234). *The Fair Puritan* certainly is an oddly overwritten tale set near Boston in 1688. Kindly Ruth lives with her stern father, ironically named Merciful, and his father, Edward Whalley the Regicide, now 80 years old. Merciful savagely beats a Native American servant whom he calls Patience although her name is Tituba. When the family learns that Charles II's agents have arrived to apprehend Goffe and Dixwell (who have already fled to New Haven), old Edward repairs to a cave 80' above their house. Governor Andros commits flamboyant cruelties (he burns the Whalley home, causes the death of Ruth's mother, tries to seduce Ruth in Boston, condemns her to death as a witch and kills Merciful). William and Mary, the new monarchs, fire the Governor so Ruth can unite with her aristocratic beau. Old Whalley, usually in a stupor, emerges from the cave and is last seen sailing with Merciful toward Boston. Although the regicide never reappears, his son duplicates the action of Hadley's Angel: just before the cowardly Governor, menaced by a group of Boston patriots, shoots Merciful to death, "a tall man dressed in black clothes rushed forward and caught his charger by the bridle." (218)

STEARNS 1847

Julius Brutus Stearns, "Hannah Duston," 1847. From an advertisement for the Tillou Gallery, Litchfield, CT, in *Antiques* 87.6 (June 1965) 629.

Pictured on page 57.

Anonymous, "The Cave of the Regicides [at West Rock in "Newhaven"]: And How Three of Them [Goffe, Whalley, Dixwell] Fared In New England." *Blackwood's Edinburgh Magazine* 61. 377 (March 1847) 333-49.

When Hawthorne spent $3.50 to tour the cave, he angrily called it "the damndest humbug in America" because "there was not even a hole in the ground deep enough to bury a dead cat" (Randall Stewart, *Nathaniel Hawthorne: A Biography* [New Haven, CT: Yale UP, 1948] 41). Clearly, however, any geographical sites associated with celebrities attracted visitors. For years, New Haven boosters mentioned the cave as a scenic wonder. See "Regicides' Cave." *The Biloxi Daily Herald* 2.226 (10 May 1900) 6, which repeats an entry from *The Detroit Free Press.*

We might compare New Haven's "hole" to the shallow caves near Mount Nonotuck, Route 116, South Hadley, Massachusetts, which supposedly sheltered Daniel Shays' protesters.

Figure 43: A cigar box from the 1880s pictured West Rock in New Haven

STERLING 1848

Charles Frederick Sterling (c. 1814-1851), *The Red Coats; or, The Sack of Unquowa. A Tale of the Revolution* (New York: Williams Brothers, 1848) 3-4.

No mention of Goffe.

Quoted on pages 42-43.

PAULDING 1849

James Kirk[e] Paulding (1778-1860), *The Puritan and His Daughter* (New York: Baker and Scribner, 1849) 2.172-73. Reprinted by Kessinger, Whitefish, MT, 2004.

The versatile Paulding was both a writer who knew Edgar Allan Poe, Washington Irving and Walt Whitman as well as Secretary of the Navy under James Monroe. Poe mentioned his "literary peculiarities" (Edgar Allan Poe, "A Chapter on Autography [Part I]." *Graham's Magazine* 19 [November 1841] 228). However, *The Puritan* is a typical early Victorian novel. In it, Indians terrify the inhabitants of a frontier town "when suddenly there appeared among them an aged man, with long white beard, and head whitened with the snows of many winters, who called on them in a voice that seemed accustomed to obedience, and arrested their retreat.... It was the last appearance of one who had sat in judgment on a king." Typical elements include the wise elder, innate authority and principled behavior. This regicide says to a young man, "I look to a new world, and a new people, to do justice to my memory.... The people who are daily flocking hither are destined to be free" (2.159). The author welded together Puritan respect for patriarchal rigor and the American Revolution's promise of individual liberty.

See Frank Davidson, "Paulding's Treatment of the Angel of Hadley." *American Literature* 7.3 (November 1935) 330-32 for a short note that summarized the plot and showed how Paulding mainly follows Stiles but has some similarities to Scott and Cooper.

CHAPMAN 1850

This dark oil painting by the former President of the Brooklyn Art Association hangs in the Forbes Library, Northampton, Massachusetts. It captures the dramatic moment when worshippers in their meeting house become aware of the native attackers in the open. The congregation on the left must briefly desert John Russell, the pastor, to follow Goffe, the warfaring Christian. Chapman arranged the participants in two contrasting ways: the whites on the left pose in classically balanced triangles; the braves rampaging outside, seen through a stage-like opening, are disordered.

Marcia Burick discussed the canvas in *A Guide to Fine Arts in the Forbes Library* (Northampton: Trustees of Forbes Library, 1994) 16-17. See also the Forbes website: www.forbes library. org. It notes, "none of this story is based in fact." The site also identifies the people.

Figure 44: Frederick A. Chapman (1818-1891), "The Angel of Hadley" or "The Perils of our Forefathers."

Chapman's painting appeared in at least two popular Victorian engravings. John C. McRae published one in New York during 1859. The contemporary advertising pamphlet offered it to the public as a reminder of Americans' "Freedom to Worship God" and as a vindication of "all contests of Anglo-Saxon faith, fortitude and prowess, with Aboriginal treachery, cruelty, and desperation." (Anonymous advertisement presumably issued at the same time as the engraving, "Illustration of an Interesting Event in the Early History of Our Country. A Beautiful Steel Engraving")

A second engraving published by Selmar Hess in New York during the 1880s unaccountably supplied Goffe with a wide-brimmed hat and took away his white beard.

Hadley artist John Gnatek adapted Chapman in a fine painting to honor the town's 300th anniversary in 1959.

Newspaper articles have discussed Chapman's painting or used it to illustrate their articles. See, "Many in 'Angel of Hadley' Painting Identified." *The Daily Hampshire Gazette* (27 July 1959); Agnes M. Dods, "The Angel of Hadley." *Amherst Journal Record* (30 July 1964) 28; John Riley, "Unearthing a Link to Town's Past." *The Daily Hampshire Gazette* (28-29 March 1992) 12; "Hidden for Years by Parson Russell, near Elmwood Hotel." (Undated and undocumented newspaper reproduction of painting's right side with Goffe in center)

George A. Snook defended the possible truth of the rescue in "Angel of Hadley. Legend or Fact." *Military Collector & Historian* 31 (1979) 11-15. He reproduced Chapman and noted that the worshippers wear authentic clothing but Goffe's costume dates from the 1620s. Also, Snook sensibly questioned why, if other military men (perhaps Major John Pynchon, Colonel Benjamin Church and Captain Gardner) were present, Goffe would have been necessary.

THE ENGLISH REGICIDES IN AMERICA 1852

"The English Regicides in America." *Chambers' Edinburgh Journal* 464 (20 November 1852) 321-24.

Recapitulation of the careers of Goffe, Whalley and Dixwell in the colonies. Begins with spirited account of defense by "a man, tall and erect of stature, calm and venerable in aspect, with long gray hair falling on his shoulders." He rallies "the bewildered and disheartened colonists," divides them into two companies, the one to fend off the direct assault, the other to outflank the "barbarous native tribe." The tactic succeeds and the "Red Men" flee. Afterward, he disappeared without identifying himself. "One or two among the people could have told who he was, but they prudently held their peace."

AMBUSH 1853

"The Ambush." Illustration by Chapin for "Scenes and Incidents in American History. No. VI. Massacre of Dickery Sargeant's Family," *The New York Journal* 5.1 (December 1853) 273 (front cover)–75.

No mention of Goffe.

Pictured and quoted on pages 44-45.

HOLLAND 1855

Josiah Gilbert Holland (1819-1881), *History of Western Massachusetts. The Counties of Hampden, Hampshire, Franklin, and Berkshire* (Springfield: Samuel Bowles, 1855) 1.119; 127-129.

A fascinating character, descended from an old Puritan family, Holland was born poor in Belchertown, became a physician who advocated a hospital for women, then wrote novels, lectured and edited *Scribner's Monthly*. He was a friend of Emily Dickinson. Holland plausibly surmised that Goffe and Whalley, "unknown to the people of Hadley, undiscovered by the soldiers billeted upon the planters, and absolutely unseen by any but Mr. Russell's family, Peter Tilton, and a Mr. Smith,

... lived for fifteen or sixteen years." His spirited retelling of the rescue dated it 12 June 1675 and provided detailed tactics: the Indians planned to invade Hadley from the south and north but were thwarted, thanks to the intervention of "a man marked in his dress, noble in his carriage, and venerable in appearance." Unfortunately, Holland assumed the palisade to the east side of West Street, built in 1676, impeded the attack.

CONNECTICUT 1855

"Connecticut." *Ballou's Pictorial Drawing-Room Companion* 9.8 (25 August 1855) cover.

No mention of Goffe.

Pictured and quoted on page 43.

BERARD 1855

Augusta Blanche Berard (1824-1901), *School History of the United States* (Philadelphia: Cowperthwaite, 1855) 30.

Quoted on page 41.

HUNTINGTON 1859

Frederic Dan Huntington (1819-1904), "Address." *Celebration of the Two Hundredth Anniversary of the Settlement of Hadley, Massachusetts at Hadley, June 8, 1859* (Northampton, MA: Bridgman and Childs, 1859) 42.

Huntington, who graduated from Amherst College and Harvard Divinity School, became the first Episcopal Bishop of Central New York. Born and died in Hadley, he often visited his family estate, the Huntington House on River Drive. Although Parson Russell's house no longer stood, Huntington reasoned from evidence provided the previous winter by an aged woman and from written sources that some physical details of the myth were credible: "Goffe saw the Indians entering the town from the mountains at a distance. Now, from Stiles' plan of Russell's house, we know that the regicide's chamber projected eastward, looking at once east, north and south.

While the people were all gone to meeting, the solitary captive would feel a degree of security in sitting at his window, which at that season might be open. There descrying the approach of the skulking savages, who would not suspect an observation from this elevated post, and who probably thought every man to be inside the meeting house, Goffe would, we may imagine, apprize the congregation at once of their danger, and throw himself in with the men as they rushed out from their interrupted devotions. Everything in this theory is consistent and probable." The easy antagonism between us and them, even in a clergyman, reflects the times.

BARTLETT c.1860

W. H. Bartlett, *The History of the United States of North America From the Discovery of the Western World to the Present Day* (New York: George Virtue, [c. 1860]): 1.155.

Dramatic notice of the salvation that emphasized the dangers of colonial living: "It was no angel, but one of Cromwell's' generals, old Goffe the regicide, who, compelled by the vigilant search made after him by order of the English government, to fly from place to place, had espied from an elevated cavern in the neighborhood the murderous approach of the savages, and hurried down to effect the deliverance of his countrymen." Fine steel engraving by James Stephenson of Edward Corbould's painting depicted Goffe in action is between pages 154-55. As Native Americans in the mid-nineteenth century resisted westward expansion and as northern suspicions grew that slave owning states employed Indian allies, such historical data found a willing audience.

JUDD 1863

Sylvester Judd (1789-1860), *The History of Hadley* (1863. Reprint. Springfield, MA.: H. R. Hunting, 1905, 211. Reprint. Somersworth, NH: New Hampshire Publishing, 1976).

Mentioned on page 68.

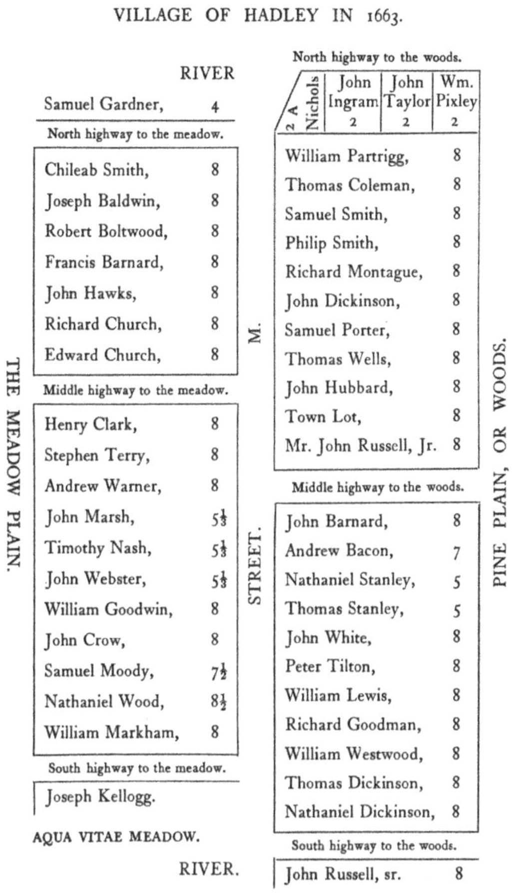

```
                    RIVER              North highway to the woods.
                                      ┌──────┬──────┬──────┬──────┐
  Samuel Gardner,      4              │      │ John │ John │ Wm.  │
                                      │Nichols│Ingram│Taylor│Pixley│
  North highway to the meadow.        │  2   │  2   │  2   │  2   │

  Chileab Smith,       8      William Partrigg,      8
  Joseph Baldwin,      8      Thomas Coleman,        8
  Robert Boltwood,     8      Samuel Smith,          8
  Francis Barnard,     8      Philip Smith,          8
  John Hawks,          8      Richard Montague,      8
  Richard Church,      8      John Dickinson,        8
  Edward Church,       8  M.  Samuel Porter,         8
                              Thomas Wells,          8
  Middle highway to the meadow.   John Hubbard,      8
                                  Town Lot,          8
  Henry Clark,         8      Mr. John Russell, Jr.  8
  Stephen Terry,       8
  Andrew Warner,       8      Middle highway to the woods.

  John Marsh,          5⅓     John Barnard,          8
  Timothy Nash,        5⅓     Andrew Bacon,          7
  John Webster,        5⅓     Nathaniel Stanley,     5
  William Goodwin,     8      Thomas Stanley,        5
  John Crow,           8      John White,            8
  Samuel Moody,        7½     Peter Tilton,          8
  Nathaniel Wood,      8½     William Lewis,         8
  William Markham,     8      Richard Goodman,       8
                              William Westwood,      8
  South highway to the meadow.    Thomas Dickinson,  8
  ┌──────────────────┐        Nathaniel Dickinson,  8
  │ Joseph Kellogg.  │
                              South highway to the woods.
  AQUA VITAE MEADOW.
                    RIVER.    John Russell, sr.      8
```

(THE MEADOW PLAIN.) — (STREET.) — (PINE PLAIN, OR WOODS.)

Figure 45: The following map appeared on page 24 of Judd's *The History of Hadley*. Compare it to the more focused sketch in Stiles 1794, Figure 34.

TUTTLE 1864

Henry Tuttle, *A Historical Compendium Comprising Important and Interesting Items in the History of the United States.* 21st edition (Portage, WI: Brannan & Turner, 1864).

Quoted on page 36. Reminded students that Whalley and Goffe "lived and died here [in Massachusetts]" without bringing up the rescue.

PALFREY 1865

John Gorham Palfrey (1796-1881), *History of New England* (Boston: Little, Brown, 1865) 3.163-65).

Stirring account of the attack by "the furious enemy" that was repulsed by, "it is said, an unknown man of advanced years." Despite the vigor of Palfrey's words ("the old ardor took possession of him once more; he rushed out to win one more victory for God's people"), he dismisses the truth of the anecdote: "I can hear of no account that is not traceable to Hutchinson's history." Despite this level-headed disclaimer, the author of Tradition Concerning General Goffe 1879 dismissed Palfrey as "romantice."

ROBBINS 1869

Chandler Robbins, "The Regicides Sheltered in New England: A Lecture of a Course by Members of the Massachusetts Historical Society, Delivered Before the Lowell Institute, Feb. 5, 1869" (Boston: John Wilson, 1869) 25-26.

Briefly retold the Angel deed from "that superstitious age" (28) and noted that it had several versions. Defended the possibility that Goffe and Whalley could have remained hidden for those fifteen years.

Quoted on page 72.

WARREN 1873

Israel Perkins Warren (1814-1892), *The Three Judges: Story of the Men who Beheaded Their King* (New York: Warren and Wyman, 1873).

A convenient history of the judges that mentioned the Angel rescue in passing: "an event which seems to be well substantiated by early and unwavering tradition" (275).

Illustration of Judge Harrison's execution on page 25.

THE ACADEMY 1874

Notes and News. *The Academy 137* (19 December 1874) 655.

Brie, confident announcement "that the old story, according to which the regicide Goffe suddenly appeared at a critical moment among the people of Hadley, Massachusetts, and led them forth to successful battle against the Indians, and then as suddenly vanished, must be unhesitatingly relegated to the region of myth. There is no contemporary evidence whatever of Goffe's presence on the occasion and it appears that the town was only alarmed, and not actually molested, by Indians."

CURTIS 1874

"Curtis. Hadley, Massachusetts." *The Indianapolis Sentinel* 22.188 (19 June 1874) 4.

A brief transcription of the closing remarks of a eulogy by George William Curtis (1824-1892), editor of *Harper's Weekly,* for Charles Sumner (1811-1874), Massachusetts senator and confidant of Lincoln. Curtis recalled that "the men of Hadley, faltering in the fierce shock of Indian battle, suddenly saw at their head the lofty form of an unknown captain, with white hair streaming on the wind, by his triumphant mien strengthening their hearts and leading them to victory."

SHELDON 1874

George Sheldon (1818-1916), "Whalley and Goffe in New England: 1660-1680. An Enquiry into the Origin of the Angel of Hadley Legend." Reprinted from the Introduction to the new edition of Sylvester Judd's *History of Hadley* (1863. Springfield, MA: H. R. Hunting, 1905). 34 pages. Originally "The Traditional Story of the Attack Upon Hadley and the Appearance of Gen. Goffe, Sept. 1, 1675: Has it any Foundation in Fact?" *The New-England Historical and Genealogical Register* 28 (October 1874) 379-91.

Although widely known, the legend, said Sheldon, is just that: a made-up plot taken from dim family anecdotes and popular desire for a rescuer. A short notice of the reprinted edition:

"Goffe and Whalley. Their Life in Hadley, Mass. – The 'Angel of Hadley' Story Disproved." *The New York Times* (19 August 1905) Book Review 54.

NASON 1874

Elias Nason (1811-87), "Hadley." *A Gazetteer of the State of Massachusetts; with Numerous Illustrations on Wood and Steel* (Boston: B. B. Russell, 1874) 239-41.

Nason, a learned clergyman, mixed geographical and esthetic information: "Mount Holyoke, 830 feet above the Connecticut River, ... is much frequented by the lovers of the beautiful." Quoted Angel account verbatim from DWIGHT 1821 without any judgment.

CAVERLY 1875

Robert Boodey Caverly (1806-87), "Dustin, Neff, and Leonardson." *Heroism of Hannah Duston, Together with the Indian Wars of New England* (Boston: B.B. Russell, 1875) 28.

No mention of Goffe. Pictured on page 57.

DEXTER 1876

Franklin B. Dexter, *Memoranda Concerning Edward Whalley and William Goffe.* [From the *Papers of the New Haven Colony Historical Society*, Vol. 2.] (New Haven: Tuttle, Morehouse & Taylor, 1876). ("Read November 14, 1870." Page 3.)

Up to its time, the most complete recording of biographical facts from published sources, diaries, court records and public documents. Cast doubt on the accuracy of Stiles 1794. Dexter's skepticism was seconded by a review in *The New-England Historical and Genealogical Register 31* (January 1877) 132-33.

Mentioned on page 67.

TROWBRIDGE 1877

Thomas R. Trowbridge, "Remarks on Mr. Dexter's Paper Respecting Whalley and Goffe." *Papers of the New Haven Colony Historical Society* 2 (1877) 147-54.

Quoted on page 76.

DEVERELL 1878

William Deverell, *The Pilgrims and the Anglican Church* [London: C. Kegan Paul, 1878] 3.

No mention of Goffe.

Quoted on pages 32.

TRADITION CONCERNING GENERAL GOFFE 1879

"Tradition Concerning General Goffe and the 'Hadley Angel.'" *History of the Connecticut Valley in Massachusetts, with Illustrations and Biographical Sketches of Some of Its Prominent Men and Pioneers* (Philadelphia: Louis H. Everts, 1876) 1.341-43.

A sympathetic retelling of the incident that postulated, "[l]ocal traditions concerning local events, whether or not sustained by known facts of history, are believed to have some occasion for their origin outside the mere imagination of men." Nevertheless, the author looked askance at highly romanticized or improbable accounts (Goffe saw that skirmishers coming from the north as he peeped out an east-facing window). Concluded reluctantly, "It is noticeable that none of the accounts respecting the 'fight' mentions the firing of a single gun, or the wounding or killing of any soldiers or savages. There is masterly to and fro, but not slaughter."

DIRECTORY 1879

Directory and Business Advertiser, of Hadley (Amherst: McCloud & Williams, 1879) 87-88.

"The fame of the regicide judges, Goffe and Whalley[,] is too well known to need mention here, but as the actual truth of their being secreted in Hadley has been questioned, the description of the rooms they occupied, by Chester Gaylord, who lived many years on the site of Mr. Russell's house[,] is subjoined." The specific measurements lent an air of reality to the concealment part of Goffe's story.

FISKE 1880

John Fiske (1842-91), *The Beginnings of New England or The Puritan Theocracy in its Relation to Civil and Religious Liberty* (Boston and New York: Houghton, Mifflin, 1880) 217-19.

A short but vigorous recreation of the rescue, with typical clichés ("yells of the Indians"; "the horrid savages"; "a stranger of reverend aspect and stately form... with an air of authority which none could gainsay") balanced by a prudent comment: "Like many other romantic stories, it rests upon insufficient authority and its truth has been called into question." Still, Fiske mused that "the supernatural explanation might have been started, with a touch of Yankee humour, as a blind."

Quoted on page 36 from the 1898 reprint.

Within the decade, Fiske briefly summarized his data in *Appletons' Cyclopedia of American Biography.* Vol. 2. Eds. James Grant Wilson and John Fiske (New York: D. Appleton, 1888) 672. This entry highlighted Goffe's intolerance (forcibly driving non-Puritans from Parliament during the Barebones Parliament and Pride's Purge), but merely mentioned the doubt about whether Goffe saved Hadley.

HADLEY'S MANY MEMORIES 1887

"Hadley's Many Memories. An Old Town Where the Nation was Born. The Fugitive Regicides and the 'Angle of Hadley' who Fought in King Philip's War." *The New York Times* (3 July 1887) 11.

A substantial elegy to Hadley's past (Goffe's exploit, Hooker's boyhood, elm-lined streets) and ominous prediction of its noisy, commerce-dominated future.

Quoted on page 90.

FISKE 1890

John Fiske, *The Beginnings of New England Or The Puritan Theocracy in its Relation to Civil and Religious Liberty* (Boston and New York: Houghton, Mifflin, 1898).

Fisk combined his belief in evolution with his admiration for the American experience.

Picture of Goffe on page 3.

HUNTINGTON 1891

Arria Sargent Huntington (1848-1954), *Under a Colonial Rooftree. Fireside Chronicles of Early New England* (Boston and New York: Houghton, Mifflin, 1891).

Daughter of Frederic Huntington the author worked for the betterment of poor women and children. This retrospective account of life at the family home, Forty Acres on River Drive, Hadley, accepted the rescue as having taken place during September 1676. Her written sources (Hutchinson, Stiles, Dwight, Scott, Cooper) seemed authentic to her because an old resident of the house told her the Angel story first communicated by "a grand-daughter of Parson Russell's third wife." The act "remains as an unquestioned tradition in the community." (12): A substantial newspaper essay repeated her belief: "Historic 'Forty Acres,.'" *The Springfield Republican* (24 July 1904) 14.

BAYNE 1892

Julia Taft Bayne (1845-1933), "Old Hadley." *The New England Magazine* 13.3 (November 1892) 329-44.

Bayne had played with Lincoln's son in the White House and later wrote a popular account of her observations. The historical article retold the Angel story and cogently defended its possibility.

Quoted on pages 73-74.

Bayne's collected poems, most published previously, appeared as *Hadley Ballads* (Chicago: Open Court, 1903). They included an account of Molly Webster, the famous Witch of Hadley, whom Margaret Atwood also recalled, and a narrative of "The Angel of Hadley."

PHILLIPS 1892

James Phillips, "William Goffe the Regicide" *The English Historical Review* 7.28 (October 1892) 717-20.

A few historical facts about Goffe's relatives and activities from letters and account books newly discovered. No record of the Angel incident.

COGSWELL 1893

Frederick Hall Cogswell, "The Regicides in New England." *The New England Magazine* 15.2 (October 1893) 188-200.

Six young men camp out in New Haven near West Rock and elect one of their group, a doctor, to retell tales of the Regicides. Standard narrative, enlivened by line drawings of the supposed grave markers of Goffe, Whalley and Dixwell, photographs of East and West Rock, plus a line drawing of the duel in Boston between one of the judges and an arrogant fencing master. The former used a cheese as a shield and a mop as his sword; with such unconventional arms, he slopped the latter's face with dirty water and warned him not to persist.

KINGSLEY 1895

Elbridge Kingsley, "Hadley." *Hadley[.] The Regicides, Indian and General History. A Souvenir in Honor of Major-General Joseph Hooker and in Anticipation of the Memorial Exercises at his Birthplace[,] Tuesday, May 7, 1895.*

Kingsley reviewed the town's history and added one interesting speculation about "the romantic episode dear to the popular heart." It probably did not take place in the village itself but southeast at Indian Hill near the Fort River. Such a site made military sense because the natives already had used it and knew an attack from Hatfield required crossing the Connecticut Rive and marching over the open meadow.

COGSWELL 1896

Frederick Hall Cogswell, *The Regicides. A Tale of Early Colonial Times* (New York: Baker & Taylor, 1896).

A prequel to Goffe's life in Hadley. Set in New Haven during winter 1661, the novel describes the effect on townspeople of the arrival of two pairs of men. Goffe and Whalley, reluctant to put their Boston and Hartford hosts in danger, plan to flee the wrath of Charles II in New York; at the same time, the royal man-hunters Thomas Kirke and Thomas Kellond appear. At one point, feather-wearing Indians kidnap the two pursuers. Cogswell incorporated material from diaries, sermons and court records to recall how everyday people plowed snow, behaved in church, taught their children in school and tried wrongdoers in court (one young woman for "filthy dalliance": hand holding, hugging and public kissing). The menace of Charles (a "jesting libertine" and liar who promised to pardon any regicides who surrendered to him) contrasts to the dignity of the fugitive patriots: Goffe is around 45, "of firm and not too heavy build, with a magnificent head rising from a strong but graceful neck and a broad pair of shoulder." Four pages from the romance's end, Goffe optimistically announces to his Connecticut benefactor, "We intend to reach Hadley in a week."

BRYANT, GAY AND BROOKS 1896

William Cullen Bryant (1794-1878), Sydney Howard Gay (1814-1888) and Noah Brooks (1830-1903), *Scribner's Popular History of the United States, From the Earliest Discoveries of the Western Hemisphere by the Northman to the Present Time, With More Than Sixteen Hundred Illustrations and Maps* (C. Scribner's Sons, 1897) 4.409-410.

Bryant, the revered poet from Cummington and relative of Hadley's blind naturalist Clarence Hawkes (1869-1954), cooperated with Sydney Howard Gay, editor of the weekly *National Anti-Slavery Standard* and, in this later edition, with Brooks, the friend and biographer of Lincoln, on an ambitious history. First issued in 1876, it balanced the appeal of adventure with the sobriety of fact: "There is no reason for doubting its [the rescue's] essential truth, though the imagination of successive narrators may have made a romance of a natural though effective incident. The regicide, Colonel Goffe, was at that period, concealed in the house of Mr. Russell at Hadley, and the old soldier certainly would not see the villagers getting the worst of the fight with the Indians if his presence and bravery could prevent it. He may have seemed to his countrymen almost a supernatural visitor when he appeared so suddenly among them, and the impression would be deepened when he as suddenly vanished. That Goffe was concealed in Hadley was probably unknown to the people, for though there was, perhaps, no wish on the part of the magistrates to surrender the regicide, had the place of the retreat of himself and Whalley been publicly known, there would have been a legal obligation for their capture not easily evaded."

JOHNSON 1897

Clifton Johnson (1865-1940), *An Unredeemed Captive. Being the Story of Eunice Williams, who, at the Age of Seven years Old, was Carried Away from Deerfield by the Indians in the Year 1704, and who Lived among the Indians in Canada as One of them the Rest of Her Life* (Holyoke, MA: Griffith, Axtell & Cady, 1897) 29.

Hadley's prolific author and historian retold Eunice's ordeal. Illustration of assault on Sheldon house in Deerfield.

Pictured on page 58.

BEVERIDGE 1900

Albert Jeremiah Beveridge (1862-1927), "In Support of an American Empire." *The Congressional Record 33* (First Session of the 56th Congress. Washington: Government Printing Office, 1900) 712.

Quoted on page 90.

WHITE 1903

Frances J. White, *Through the Old-time Haunts of the Norwottuck and Pocumtuck Indians* (Springfield: F. A. Bassett, 1903) 14-16.

Sprightly guide to Hadley and its neighbors for those interested in a trolley tour. Asserted, "Everyone knows the legend of the 'Angel of Hadley' ... Some give it credence; other pronounce it a myth; still others favor it somewhat but 'do not know.'"

TOM QUICK 1904

Theodore D. Schoonmaker, "Tom Quick. The Indian Slayer, or The Avenger of the Delaware." http://www.jrbooksonline.com Accessed 25 November 2009.

Basis for remark on page 58.

WOODWARD 1905

P. Henry Woodward, "The True Story of the Regicides." *Connecticut Magazine* 9.3 (1905) 539-48.

Repetition of Stiles, written for a popular audience, with little historical validity.

Figure 46: Goffe at Hadley 1906
James Wilford Garner (1871-1938) and Henry Cabot Lodge (1850-1924), *The History of the United States* (Philadelphia: John D. Morris, 1906) 1.176.

GOFFE AT HADLEY 1906

"Goffe at Hadley." Artist: A. R. Ward. Engraver: Anthony Varick Stout (1835-1906). In William Cullen Bryant, Sydney Howard Gay and Noah Brooks, *Scribner's Popular History of the United States, From the Earliest Discoveries of the Western Hemisphere by the Northman to the Present Time, With More Than Sixteen Hundred Illustrations and Maps* (C. Scribner's Sons, 1897) 4.410.

Garner, the academic historian, and Lodge, the conservative senator from Massachusetts and champion of the Anglo-Saxon "race," briefly noted the rescue: "An attack on Hadley, according to tradition, was repelled under the leadership of an aged man commonly believed to have been Goff, one of the regicides who had found a refuge in America." The uncritical acceptance of Goffe's role nicely illustrated Lodge's respect for elite Anglo-Saxon men of action who battled less advanced peoples.

WALKER 1906

Alice Morehouse Walker, *Historic Hadley. A Story of the Making of a Famous Massachusetts Town* (New York: Grafton, 1906) 26-27.

Brief reminder of the rescue tempered by the assertion that "the modern historian discovered that Hadley was not attacked that day, September 1675, and that the story is based only upon a tradition which has no real foundation."

ROBERTS 1906

George S. Roberts, *Historic Towns of the Connecticut River Valley* (Schenectady, NY: Robson & Adee, 1906) 352-353.

An energetic retelling of the rescue. Two years before (10 September 1674), "strange noises were heard, like the discharge of great cannon, and the earth shook so that everyone was terrified." Sure enough, these omens preceded the nearly fatal battle by 700 Indians, which Roberts dated 12 June 1676, "according to Barber." He made no mention of a church service, treating the attack as ongoing until "Goff, one of the regicides, a man of commanding and venerable presence, and an experienced soldier, came from concealment in the home of the Rev. John Russell, and revived the flagging energy and courage of the settlers." In this version, "Goff" discharged a cannon that discomfited the Natives long enough so Major Talcott from Northampton could reinforce the town. The whites then drove the raiders back into the wood. Chapter contains a nice photograph of the tree-shaded "Regicide House" (348), formerly on West Street and state route 9, now marked by a commemorative boulder.

Bliss Carman (1861-1929), "The Spirit in Arms. (An Incident of 1675)." *Collier's* 40.22 (22 February 1908) 2.

The once well-known Canadian poet recalled "Goffe the regicide" who "had seen from his place of hiding / The redskins creeping down, / Malignant shapes in the shadows. / On the unoffending town." He perpetuated the usual contrast between "sleepy Hadley … this lovely Puritan town" and "Indian pillage and raid" by "the stealthy foe." Goffe recreated his former service in England: "The intrepid soldier of justice / Once more had unsheathed his sword / To defend the rights of a people, / Ere he passed to the great reward." He was, in Carman's poem, obviously one of the Elect.

The Spirit in Arms
(An Incident of 1675)
by BLISS CARMAN

WHEN the just ire of England
Arose in daring might
Against the perfidious Stuart,
To uphold a diviner right,
"Let kings learn," said her Commons,
"Their duty once for all,"
And sent the Lord's anointed
To the headsman of Whitehall.

BUT strange are the shifts for freedom,
Heavy tradition's hand,
And the days of the avenger
Were not long in the land.
No sooner another Stuart
Was safe on the throne once more,
Than his father's judges were outlawed,
Hunted from door to door.

TWO oversea for safety
To wild New England fled,
To haunt her forest borders,
With a price upon each head.
Harried from hiding to hiding,
Eating their bread in haste,
By many a hearth and camp-fire
Their unresting trail was traced.

TO-DAY in sleepy Hadley,
In its wide, green-shaded street,
They will point you out a dwelling
Was the regicides' retreat.
Here between ranks of homesteads
Their public common was made
For pasture and pleasure, protected
From Indian pillage and raid.

DEEP in the needing greensward
The arching elm trees stand,
Under the blue of August,
With peace over all the land.
On such a day in summer
Seasons and seasons ago,
On this lovely Puritan haven
Descended the stealthy foe.

THE people were all at worship,
When a sudden fiendish yell
Broke on the fast-day stillness;
They knew what it meant full well.
Forth rushed the men from the meeting
(Armed were they always then),
To find their quiet Main Street
Swarming with painted men.

TRAPPED, for the instant panic
Unmanning the stoutest there,
Drove them back to the doorway;
Disaster was in the air.
They saw their wives and children
Given to knife and brand,
And the blood ran back for a moment
From every hardy hand.

MAZED by the din and horror,
Stampeded by savage war,
Where was the spirit that triumphed
At Naseby and Dunbar?
Suddenly there before them,
Taking command, was seen
A thrilling resolute presence,
With heroic right in his mien.

AT the call of that confident leader
Their sickened hearts grew bold,
And they thought how the Lord had smitten
The Midianites of old.
Then did the Puritan spirit
Come back to them where they stood,
And they fell on the shrieking Nipmucks
And drove them back to the wood.

BUT when the rout was over,
Ere the sweat was wiped away
From the tanned and toil-worn faces
In thankfulness that day,
They turned to behold the stranger
Who had saved them from worse than death,
And the spirit in arms had vanished,
He had come and gone like a breath.

HAD they but looked on a vision?
Or, seeing them too sore tried,
Had the Lord sent His angel among them?
It was Goffe the regicide.
He had seen from his place of hiding
The redskins creeping down,
Malignant shapes in the shadows,
On the unoffending town.

AND quick to the call of outrage,
He who could have no part
In the open life of his fellows
Had come to strengthen their heart.
The intrepid soldier of justice
Once more had unsheathed his sword
To defend the rights of a people,
Ere he passed to the great award.

Figure 47: Bliss Carman (1861-1929), "The Spirit in Arms. (An Incident of 1675)." Collier's 40.22 (22 February 1908) 2.

Carman decided to move from New Brunswick to Connecticut in 1909. The dating of the poem may indicate that plans for Hadley's 250th anniversary in 1909 had already reached New Canaan.

Figure 48: To accompany Carman's "Spirit," George Wright supplied this stirring illustration on page 1.

Figure 49: Clarence Hawkes (1869-1954), designer, "Hadley's Angel[.] Goffe the Regicide." Photo Courtesy of the Hadley Historical Society

This float, the third of twelve designed by the blind naturalist Clarence Hawkes, enlivened the festivities for Hadley's 250th anniversary celebration. During four days (1-4 August), practically everyone participated in church services, speeches, dances, a fireman's muster, flag raising, a baseball game and, most notably, this parade of floats. Hawkes' inventiveness—he had never seen a float before he was accidentally blinded at age 13—won praise from big-city newspapers. (*The Boston Daily Globe*, 18 July 1909, page 41; 5 August 1909, page 9; *The New York Times*, 5 August 1909, page 7; *Springfield Daily Republican*, 5 August 1909, page 10.) The image of Chapman's Goffe appeared on the cover and on page 7 of the official souvenir book, *Historic Hadley[.] Quarter Millennial Souvenir[,]* 1659-1909. Ed. Clifton Johnson (Northampton: Souvenir, 1909). The Angel's likeness also decorated an advertising folder, "Hadley Facts," the Eastman-Tilton family reunion badge, a celluloid pin (with General Hooker on the reverse) and a receipt form for those who contributed money "to the honor and glory of Old Hadley." The remarkable festival did not feature the contributions of recent arrivals, but it did provide a vibrant lesson in civic cooperation and communal memory.

MARSHALL 1917

Henrietta Elizabeth Marshall (1876-?), *This Country of Ours; The Story of the United States* (New York: George H. Doran, 1917) Part III, Chapters 31-32.

A simplified narrative of the hunt for the Regicides and King Philip's War. Detailed description of the "safe retreat" in Parson Russell's attic that concealed Goffe and Whalley. Marshall prefaced Angel's appearance with typical clichés. Native Americans "kept to their old ways of fighting, and, stealthily as wild animals, they skulked behind trees, or lurked in the long grass, seeking their enemies." In contrast to "this red terror," white settlers "went on quietly with their daily life. On week days they tilled their fields and minded their herds, on Sundays they went, as usual, to church."

BOLTON 1919

Charles Knowles Bolton, *Portraits of Persons Born Abroad Who Came to the Colonies in North America Before the Year 1701. With an Introduction, Biographical Outlines and Comments on the Portraits* (Boston: The Boston Athenaeum, 1919) 2.393-395.

Brief resume of Goffe's life with interesting quotations from his letters. The relevant mention of the rescue is on page 393: "In September, 1675, Goffe is said to have emerged from hiding to lead the settlers against the Indians, but the story is of doubtful value. His last letter is dated 2 April, 1679, and no trace of him is found after that year."

Picture of Goffe on page 3.

COPELAND 1924 (?)

Elmer H. Copeland, "The Angel of Hadley[.] Major General William Goffe[,] One of the Judges of King Charles the First. Being a Reply to ... George Sheldon." Typed MS, 138 pages, probably 1924. In author's possession.

A sincere but not altogether successful attempt to rehabilitate the veracity of the story. Overstated and used late oral traditions.

WELLES 1927

Lemuel Aiken Welles, *The History of the Regicides in New England* (New York: Grafton Press, 1927) 21.

Conventional retelling of the Angel incident.

ORIANS 1932

G. Harrison Orians, "The Angel of Hadley in Fiction[.] A Study of the Sources of Hawthorne's 'The Grey Champion.'" *American Literature* 4 (1932) 257-69.

A convenient listing of many early nineteenth-century uses of the Angel's rescue.

JOHNSON 1932

Clifton Johnson, *Historic Hampshire in the Connecticut Valley. Happenings in a Charming Old New England County from the Time of the Dinosaur Down to About 1900* (Springfield: Milton Bradley, 1932) 97-98.

With clarity but not much historical authority, Johnson described the regicides' hiding place in the Russell home: "The Judges occupied a spacious chamber in the second story of the parsonage with the joists and flooring of the garret showing above. North of the big chimney was a closet that afforded a passage to another chamber, and one of the broad boards in its floor was not fastened down. By slipping this lengthwise a few inches, one could be raised to allow a person to lower himself into the space below. Then the board could be replaced." According to legend, officers of the Crown walked through the passage above their heads.

WELLES 1935

The Regicides in Connecticut (New Haven, CT: Yale UP, 1935).

Condensed version of Welles 1927 for the Connecticut Tercentenary Pamphlet Series, # 35. Critical of Stiles.

Mentioned on page 67.

MARLOWE 1945

George Francis Marlowe, *Coaching Roads of Old New England* (New York: Macmillan, 1945).

Typical local color account of the rescue concluding, "Some thought that an angel in the form of an old man had been sent from Heaven. A few who had known Goffe believed that it was he who had been their deliverer." (102)

OSTERWEIS 1953

Rollin G. Osterweis, *Three Centuries of New Haven, 1638-1938* (New Haven: Yale University Press, 1953).

Critical of Stiles.

Mentioned on page 67.

DOUBLEDAY 1962

Nathaniel Hawthorne, *Tales of His Native Land.* Ed. Neal F. Doubleday (Boston: Heath, 1962).

Suggested one more possible source for "The Gray Champion" in addition to Goffe: William Tudor's "An Address Delivered to the Phi Beta Kappa Society." See Tudor 1815.

WINSTON 1964

Alexander Winston, "The Hunt for the Regicides." *American Heritage* 16 (December 1964) 26-29, 90-93.

Popular and nicely illustrated summary of the fugitive judges' activities in New England. Winston said, "The story of the gray-bearded Goffe's sudden appearance as if from nowhere to lead the men of Hadley, Massachusetts, against attacking Indians may not be completely legendary."

WHO WAS 1971

"Who Was the Real Angel of Hadley." *The Daily Hampshire Gazette* (7 April 1971).

Brief recital of regicides' exile and purported rescue from attack. Anonymous author concluded that the real angel was Parson Russell because he gave up his autonomy to shelter his comrades.

BELL 1971

Michael Davitt Bell, *Hawthorne and the Historical Romance of New England* (Princeton, NJ: Princeton UP, 1971) 26-53.

Discussed the figure of the regicide in Scott and Cooper. Hawthorne transformed it in "The Gray Champion" into "the 'type' not of the future but of the past, not of 1776 but of 'New England's *hereditary* spirit.'" Hawthorne saw the Champion as a model for his countrymen: "self-reliance emerges when outsiders threaten to reduce New Englanders to subordination."

DAVIS 1973

Joseph A. Davis, "The Oldest Puritan: A Study of the Angel of Hadley Legend in Hawthorne's 'The Gray Champion.'" *Rackham Literary Studies* 4 (1973) 25-44.

Provided full quotations from sources and decided that the mythopoeic energy of New Englanders manufactured a typical savior hero who would validate their respect for both group worth and individual initiative. Davis interestingly mentioned Jacob Grimm's *Teutonic Mythology* (1844. English translation of *Deutsche Mythologie*, 1835), where vanished defenders like Siegfried, Charlemagne, Frederick Barbarossa, King Arthur and Robert the Bruce share traits: each has been banished or apparently died; common people still honor and await him; he dwells for a time in a cave; when he reappears, he is old, with a long white beard; he often defeats an enemy; sometimes, the battle signals the end of the world.

NEWBERRY 1976

Fred Newberry, "'The Gray Champion': Hawthorne's Ironic Criticism of the Puritan Rebellion." *Studies in Short Fiction* 13 (1976) 363-70.

Although the Champion seems to incarnate positive virtues, Hawthorne mentions Puritan slaughters of Native Americans, thus undercutting a simple response to the Champion's heritage.

BRUMM 1976

Ursula Brumm, "A Regicide Judge as 'Champion' of American Independence." *Amerikastudien* 21 (1976) 177-86.

Questioned the facts – how could two men hide for so long in a close-knit village? But the legend obviously appealed to a specific regional audience because it recalled how a pious Puritan could flee tyranny, survive dangers and help his own people. Brumm theorized that the Angel, as molded by Hawthorne, "represents the two conflicting elements of the Puritan self, the rebellious and the authoritarian part"; further, "his Champion suggests not only the ideal but also the violent and bloody implications of the republican spirit and of revolution."

SNOOK 1979

George Snook, "Angel of Hadley[:] Legend or Fact." *Military Collector & Historian* 31 (1979) 11-15.

Attempted to moderate Sheldon by postulating that "[l]egends generally have some basis in fact.... [I]t does appear as though General Goffe could have made an appearance in Hadley at that date." Mentioned Frederick Cartwright's nineteenth-century oil painting "The Perils of Our Forefathers" in the Forbes Library, Northampton. See Chapman 1850.

WILSON 1981

Douglas C. Wilson, "The Angel of Hadley." *The Country Side Magazine* 1 (Winter 1981-82) 10-14, 16-17, 66-67, 69, 94.

A lucid recitation of the data in popular form.

DEKKER 1983

George Dekker, "Sir Walter Scott, the Angel of Hadley, and American Historical Fiction." *Journal of American Studies* 17 (1983) 211-27.

A detailed study of the ways that Scott, Cooper and Hawthorne transformed the Angel story. For example, Scott offered alternate possibilities to explain the unexpected deliverer (supernatural being, a champion, a recluse). In addition, Scott enlarged Goffe from a local champion who impressed his contemporaries to a deliverer who would, like Arthur and Holger the Dane, reappear when his whole country needed him.

DUNN 1983

Jack Dunn, *The Diary of General William Goffe* (np: The Book Press, 1983). Serialized in *The Valley Advocate* (Winter 1991-1992).

The entertaining novel briefly mentioned the Angel's rescue and the Chapman painting in Northampton's Forbes Library. Rich with references to Valley landmarks, restaurants and roads, it followed the adventures of a wealthy young lawyer whose family has inherited the Hadley house that sheltered Goffe. He and his Mount Holyoke girlfriend search for Goffe's diary and secret documents supposedly burned in Governor Hutchinson's Boston home during the Revolution. Like other fictional hunts for the Ark of the Covenant or the Holy Grail, this playful beginning leads to terror: a ghost's appearance, secret chambers and murder. Dunn sued Dan Brown, saying the latter's *Da Vinci Code* (2003) plagiarized his *The Vatican Boys* (1997).

WILSON 1987

Douglas C. Wilson, "Web of Secrecy: Goffe, Whalley, and the Legend of Hadley." *The New England Quarterly* 60 (1987) 515-48.

THE go-to essay if you wish to believe that Goffe really saved the town from destruction by the Indians. Wilson cogently retold the facts and alleged facts, reasonably pointing out that "[t]he regicide possessed three qualities that appealed to romantic sensibilities: antiquity, national spirit, and individualism." Also, Stiles supplied the supernatural ingredient. By the 1870s, the literary taste for realism allowed the Angel story to fade except as a specimen of antiquarian excitement. Wilson showed how authors accepted as true the basic plot. They may have readjusted dates of Indians skirmishes to create a heroic tale that covertly criticized the unjust monarchy. Successors of Charles I had long memories and an appetite for revenge. Late seventeenth-century Americans would have expressed their praise of a regicide in roundabout ways. Wilson thus defended the basic truth of the tale: colonialists united in their resistance to the motherland and may have concealed Goffe, whether or not he repulsed an Indian attack.

Mentioned on page 74.

WILSON 1991

Douglas C. Wilson, Review of Russell Bourne, *The Red King's Rebellion: Racial Politics in New England, 1675-1678* (New York: Atheneum, 1990). *The New England Quarterly* 64.1 (March 1991) 71-74.

Wilson's largely negative review of Bourne's history usefully pointed out that the Angel story was not "a Puritan fabrication" because "no Puritan wrote about it at all."

SARGENT 1992

Mark L. Sargent, "Thomas Hutchinson, Ezra Stiles, and the Legend of the Regicides." *William and Mary Quarterly* 49 (1992) 413-48.

A close reading that argued the royalist Hutchinson denigrated Goffe as a rebel who paid the just price of being exiled from his own kind. In contrast, Stiles attempted to save Goffe's dignity because the Puritan participated in a social movement similar to our current Revolutionary War. Sargent saw the competing political philosophies of Tory and Whig in several other American works that adopted the regicide figure.

SARGENT 1993

Mark L. Sargent, "The Witches of Salem, the Angel of Hadley, and the Friends of Philadelphia." *American Studies 34 (1993)* 105-20.

Discussed the common linkage of a regicide hero and witch hunts in Mchenry 1823, Barker 1824 and *The Witch of New England* 1828. These works protested Puritan violence toward fellow villagers based on supernatural evidence.

DEMOS 1995

John Demos, *The Unredeemed Captive* (New York: Vintage, 1995) 3.

No mention of Goffe. Quoted on page 28.

LUTZ 1998

Cora E. Lutz, "Ezra Stiles and the Legend of the Angel of Hadley." *Yale University Library Gazette* 73 (1998) 115-23.

A short, clear account of how Stiles gathered his evidence from written and oral sources. Also Lutz asserted that Chapman's painting followed Stiles' account.

APPLETON 1999

John Appleton, "Tale of 'Angel of Hadley' Has Roots With Regicides." *Union News* [Springfield, MA] (5 May 1999) A12.

A quick retelling of the story that "has been treated as history, legend and mere myth."

FREEMAN 2003

James A. Freeman, "William Goffe, the Angel of Hadley." *Massachusetts Center for Renaissance Studies Newsletter* (Autumn 2003) 9.

Brief summary of address delivered at "Hadley in the Renaissance. A Conference on Hadley in the 17th Century" organized by the Hadley Historical Commission, coordinated by Marla Miller and Margaret Freeman, 3 May 2003. This monograph contains all the information presented there. The *Newsletter* 13-16 also contains a summary of Martin Antonetti, "Tracing the Hadley Bible," a compelling demonstration that Dorothy Russell, wife of Reverend John Russell, who sheltered the regicides, owned the so-called Goffe Bible. For Antonetti's full article, see "The 'Goffe Bible': Succor for the Regicides?" *Cultivating a Past. Essays on the History of Hadley, Massachusetts.* Ed. Marla R. Miller (Amherst: University of Massachusetts Press, 2009) 121-134.

LANCTO 2004

Craig Lancto, "The Angel of Hadley: Extraordinary Events in the French and Indian Wars." *The World and I* 19.2 (February 2004) 178-84.

A recital of the facts surrounding the attacks on Hadley and the 1704 raid on Deerfield. Mentioned the roles of Native Americans but took no stand on "[w]hether the dramatic intervention of the Angel of Hadley was a startling phenomenon or apocryphal."

ANGELO 2004

Holly Angelo, "Historic 'Angel' Touched Hadley." *The Republican* [Springfield, MA] (1 May 2004) B2.

Brief report on the talk by Judge W. Michael Ryan at Hadley's Eastern Hampshire District Court, located on route 9 near the site of John Russell's house. Ryan said the genuineness of Goffe's deed isn't the issue because "the worth of a story is not dependent on its truth."

WILSON 2006

Douglas C. Wilson, "The Legend of a Grateful Ghost." *Daily Hampshire Gazette* (31 October 2006) A6.

Brief account of the Regicides' time in Hadley with the emphasis upon Whalley's unknown burial site. He apparently died after a stroke sometime in the early 1670s and may have been placed in a makeshift vault in Parson Russell's cellar. Workers who dismantled part of the parsonage in 1795 found a few bones that might have belonged to the aged general.

BELLANGER 2008

Jeff Bellanger, "The Angel of Hadley." *Weird Massachusetts* (New York: Sterling, 2008) 19-20.

A short retelling of the legend. Information supplied by James A. Freeman, who believes the salvation from Indian attack incident is a later invention.

STORROW 2009

Ben Storrow, "The Angel of Hadley: Fact, Fiction or Both?" "Town of Hadley 350th Anniversary[,] 1659-2009." Supplement to *The Daily Hampshire Gazette* & *Amherst Bulletin* (4-5 June 2009) 20-21.

A focused questioning of the rescue. Both authorities whom Storrow interviewed, James A. Freeman and Katire Krol, Head of Forbes Library's Information Services, agreed that Goffe spent time hidden in Hadley but probably did not foil an Indian attack.

SETTLERS 2009

Aron Heller, "Settlers Protest in Jerusalem against Construction Freeze." *The Boston Globe* (10 December 2009) A24.

Article and picture of sign-carrying citizens who object to their government's ban against building in Palestinian neighborhoods.

Mentioned on page 91.

FREEMAN 2009

Eric N. Freeman, *Hadley in the Civil War* (Amherst: White River Press, 2009).

A narrative that documented all known soldiers from Hadley. Suggested that John Dunbar, who lived on West Street, graduated from Hopkins Academy and Amherst College, then became an authority on the Pawnees, inspired John Dunbar, the fictional hero of Michael Blake's *Dances With Wolves.*

Mentioned on page 1.

GOFFE RALLYING HADLEY RESIDENTS NO DATE

Anonymous depiction of Goffe Rallying Hadley Residents to Resist the Indian Attack. www.sonofthesouth.net/revolutionary-war/pilgrims/king-philips-war.jp Accessed 22 March 2009.

Pictured on page 78.

HANNAH DUSTON NO DATE

"Hannah Duston's Escape from Contoocook Island, New Hampshire (now known as Dustin Island) on the night of March 29th-30th, 1697." http://www.hawthorneinsalem.org/images/image.php?name=MMD1506 Accessed 6 May 2009.

Pictured on page 56.

GOFF NO DATE

John W. Goff, "A Time-Line Researched by John W. Goff for Major General William Goffe, Supported by the Factual Sources." http://genforum.genealogy.com/goff Accessed 1 April 2009.

GENEALOGICAL DATA

A useful compendium of genealogical data, reproduced in its original form below.

1.1604: Parents: Rev Stephen Goffe, Rector of Stanmer, Sussex, England and Deborah West; married 7 May 1604. (FHL IGI Index for Sussex)

2.1605-1626: Five sons born to Stephen & Deborah Goffe:

Stephen (1605-1681); John (1610?-1661); William (1614-1679-80?); James (-1656); Timothie (1626-). Sources: (DNB Goffe pp.69-74; Burkes Peerage & Baronetage, 99th ed. (1949) pp 838; Eng. Hist Rev. (1892) vol vii pp 717-720; FHL IGI Index for Sussex.)

3.1634: William Goffe apprenticed July 15, 1634 to the Grocer, William Vaughn in London. Source: (Temple, RKG; The English Regicides (1988) pp A-24. Guildhall Library, London, Guildhall MS. 11593/1 f.48.)

4.1642: William Goffe arrested and imprisoned in London for petitioning for Parliament's control of the civilian militia: (DNB, William Goffe, pp 71.)

5.1642-43: William Goffe; quartermaster in a regiment of Foot in 1642; (Wood, Anthony, Fausti oxoniensis, 2nd pt. 1642-1691 (1820 ed) pp136.) In 1643 Goffe was captain in Barclay's regiment of Foot. (Firth & Davies, Regimental History of Cromwell's Army, (1940) vol 1, pp 359). Goffe captain in Harley's regiment of Foot in 1645; (Spriggs Army List of 1645)

6.1645? –1650: William Goffe married to Frances Whalley, dau of Col. Edward Whalley, before 1650, exact date unknown; (Jagger, G. The Fortunes of the Whalley Family of Screvton Notts (1973) pp114, fn 2 PRO) The daughters born to this marriage were: Elizabeth, Frances, Judith (Coll Mass Hist. Soc. (1868) 4th ser. Vol viii pp 122-225) ; and a son, Richard, (Burkes Peerage & Baronetage, 99th ed. (1949) pp 838).

7.1647: William Goffe made Lt. Colonel; (Woodhouse, ASP; Puritanism and Liberty, pp19)

8.1649: William Goffe appointed a judge in the trial of King Charles I and signs the death warrant. (Ashley, M. Cromwell's Generals, (1954) pp 160.)

9.1649-50: William Goffe stationed in London guarding Whitehall. (Cal.State Papers Domestic: 1649-50)

10.1650: Lt Col William Goffe appointed to Cromwell's staff for the Scottish Campaign (Firth & Davies Reg Hist Cromwell's Army (1940) pp 329.) Made full Colonel and given command of the Ironsides Foot. (Ibid pp 330)

11.1653: Daughter, Frances, born Dec 11, 1653 in London. (CFI LDS London P001601 36796)

12.1655: Col. William Goffe made Major General by Cromwell for governing Sussex, Hampshire, and Berkshire: (Hill, C. Cromwell pp 145; Thurloe Papers (1742) vol IV)

13.1656: Maj Gen William Goffe elected to Parliament from Hampshire: (State Papers John Thurloe, vol V pp 329)

14.1657: William Goffe appointed to Cromwell's House of Lords and made William. Lord Goffe. (State Papers John Thurloe, vol II, pp668)

15.1658: Wiiliam, Lord Goffe granted lands in Ireland by Richard Cromwell. (State Papers John Thurloe, vol VII pp 504)

16.1660, May: Charles II restored to the throne of England; Goffe and Whalley take ship for Boston, Mass Bay Colony. (Welles, LA; History of the Regicides in New England (1927) pp 23-24.)

17.1661, Feb 26; Goffe and Whalley leave Boston for New Haven, Conn and reside with Rev. John Davenport and others. (Welles,

LA; History of the Regicides in New England (1927) pp31). Aug 19th they moved to Micah Thomkin's house and resided with him for two years. (Ibid pp 58).

18.1664. Oct 13: Goffe and Whalley left New Haven and traveled to Hadley, Mass. where they resided with Rev. John Russell. (Ibid pp 74; Stiles, Ezra; History of Three of the Judges of King Charles ! (1794) pp 26 ; Welles, LA; History of the Regicides in New England (1927) pp 74).

19.1665, Feb.: Goffe and Whalley visited for six weeks in Hadley by the regicide, Col John Dixwell (Welles, LA; History of the Regicides in New England (1927) pp 75).

20. 1671-Apr 1678; William Goffe continues his correspondence from Hadley with his wife, Frances Goffe, in England, and with others, some twelve letters surviving, William's and Frances's letters attesting to the deep and sincere love for each other that nothing could diminish. (Coll Mass Hist. Soc. (1868) 4th ser. Vol viii pp 122-225)

21.1674-5; Edward Whalley dies; Hadley attacked by Indians and Goffe rallies the citizens in defending their town. (Thomas Hutchinson Papers (1865) vol 2 pp 188-9; Judd, S. *History of Hadley* (1905) pp 138)

22.1676, July; Goffe leaves Hadley and travels to Hartford and lives with Thomas Bull. (Welles, L. History of the Regicides in New England (1927) pp 98).

23.1678, Goffe recognized in Hartford and nearly arrested but escapes. (Welles pp 101-102; Proc Mass Hist Soc. (1856) Vol III, Ser I, pp 60-63)

24.1679-80; Goffe simply disappears and no reliable record of his fate or whereabouts is ever found. It is presumed by some that he died, however many rumors of his whereabouts surface and persist. (Whalley, S. English Record of the Whalley Family (1901) pp 76-79; Dwight, Timothy; Travels in New England and New York (1822) Vol I pp 256; Stiles, Ezra: History of the Three Judges (1794) Chap IV; Proc Mass Hist Soc (1879-80) Vol XVII, Ser I)

HADLEY

1659-2009

350 YEARS

www.ingramcontent.com/pod-product-compliance
Lightning Source LLC
Chambersburg PA
CBHW030933090426
42737CB00007B/417